THE
ROCK GARDEN

GAIL HARLAND

AMBERLEY

For Ash and Jonathan, with love always

First published 2025

Amberley Publishing
The Hill, Stroud,
Gloucestershire, GL5 4EP

www.amberley-books.com

Copyright © Gail Harland, 2025

The right of Gail Harland to be identified as the Author
of this work has been asserted in accordance with the
Copyright, Designs and Patents Act 1988.

ISBN: 978 1 3981 1992 5 (print)
ISBN: 978 1 3981 1993 2 (ebook)

British Library Cataloguing in Publication Data.
A catalogue record for this book is available from the British Library.

Typeset in 10pt on 13pt Celeste.
Typesetting by SJmagic DESIGN SERVICES, India.
Printed in the UK.

EU GPSR Authorised Representative
Appointed EU Representative: Easy Access System Europe Oü, 16879218
Address: Mustamäe tee 50, 10621, Tallinn, Estonia
Contact Details: gpsr.requests@easproject.com, +358 40 500 3575

Contents

1

Rock Around the Clock

Rock Gardens Through Time

The Canadian author Margaret Atwood said in *Two-Headed Poems*, 'This is the rock garden. In it, the stones too are flowers.' The attraction rock gardens hold for many people is the combination of solid, permanent stone with the ephemeral beauty of flowers. Rock gardens appeal to both plant enthusiasts and those with an interest in geology or the sculptural properties of stone. Individual stones are as varied as plants, often seeming to have great personality. The strata of sedimentary rocks are endlessly fascinating. Successful rock gardens depend on skilful use of stone to create an aesthetically pleasing design and a suitable habitat for plants.

Rocks have been used as decorative and symbolic elements in Chinese gardens for thousands of years. During the Shang dynasty (1600–1046 BC) in the Yellow River valley, the site of China's most ancient civilization, gardens held collections of ornamental plants, birds and animals as well as fruit and vegetables. They were enclosed spaces, creating an idealised landscape of rocks, water and plants. They served as displays of status for the imperial families and as places of retreat and contemplation for poets and scholars.

In Chinese culture the mountain is esteemed as an unchanging presence, symbolising the preservation of order and stability. There is a fascination with unusually shaped rocks, seen to express individuality and originality and reflecting the legendary mountains with hanging gardens that feature in the mythology of Buddhism. Particularly valued are bizarre, naturally moulded limestone rocks formed by erosion, such as those found around Taihu Lake in Suzhou, with preference given to tall, thin stones with many cavities and holes and a rich surface texture.

The Japanese too have revered rocks from ancient times. Rocks were thought to possess spirits and to attract benevolent beings to earth. The fantastical shapes admired by the Chinese had less importance than what was considered the natural essence of stones. Appreciation of the aesthetic values of small expressive stones, known as *suiseki*, dates from the reign of Suiko (593–628), the first reigning empress of Japan, who received gifts of treasured rocks from the Chinese imperial court. *Sakuteiki*, a mid-eleventh-century

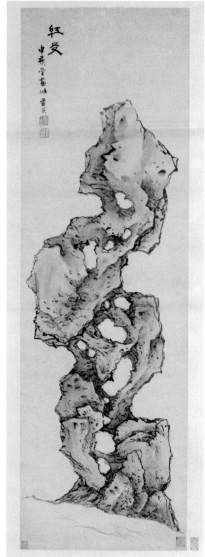

Above left: *A Colorful Spring* by Giuseppe Castiglione (1688–1766). (National Palace Museum, Taipei)

Above right: This portrait of a rock by the seventeenth-century Chinese artist Lan Ying is called *Red Friend* and is an example of the strangely faceted rocks treasured by Chinese collectors. (The Metropolitan Museum of Art, New York)

treatise on gardening written by the courtier and poet Tachibana Toshitsuna, discussed the placing of stones by listening to their natural desires. It recommended a *karesansui* (Japanese dry garden) if there were no natural lake or stream, using meticulously arranged rocks and pruned plants to create a miniature stylized landscape. Areas of raked gravel or sand represent ripples in water. Daily maintenance of the garden was considered to be good discipline and training for meditation.

Japanese garden with rocks and raked gravel. (Image by Kip Ferguson/Pixabay)

In Europe the botanical garden of the University of Padua, Italy, was founded in 1545. In 1552 a wall was built around the garden to prevent theft of valuable plants. Today the rockery there exhibits examples of typical alpine plants including edelweiss (*Leontopodium alpinum*) and *Campanulas* and a collection of local plants from the Euganean Hills. The Montpellier Botanical Garden in France was created in 1593 by Pierre Richer de Belleval, physician to Henri IV. Belleval undertook plant-hunting trips to the Alps and Pyrenees and swapped plants with other botanists. He constructed a mount described by Thomas Platter in 1598 as:

> An artificial mountain made of terraces in tiers allows at one time culture and presentation of plants to visitors. Its orientation from east to west and its height determine two exposures: the one to the north devoted to plants that come from wooded lands and forests; the other to the south where bushes, thorny or not, and plants from the copse grow at the same time. The path from the summit is the destiny of plants from sunny, rocky, and sandy places being in every way much more dry and exposed than the lower levels.

Early mounts such as that at the Château de Gaillon in Normandy often had allegorical associations, referencing Mount Parnassus in Greece, supposedly home to the god Apollo. More prosaically they also provided exercise and views of the garden or surrounding countryside. The mount at New College, Oxford, was in progress in 1594 and a Parnassus mound was created at Richmond for Prince Henry in 1615. The artificial mound in the grounds of Marlborough College has prehistoric origins. It was reused as the motte for the castle keep and subsequently became part of a seventeenth-century landscaping scheme by the Earl of Hertford. The mount was crowned with a gazebo and in 1723 William Stukeley recorded a flint and stone grotto cut into the base.

A rock garden for alpine plants in Verrières-le-Buisson, near Paris in France, around 1909.

The Grade II listed shell house, grotto and rockery at Bicton Park in Devon date from 1845.

During the Age of Enlightenment many people became interested in the scientific study of plants. Dr John Fothergill (1712–80) graduated from Edinburgh University, moving to London to practise medicine. He worked long hours and his leisure time was taken up with causes including prison reform and poor relief but he still found time to study botany, supporting several botanical expeditions. Fothergill would waive his medical fees for patients if they could offer him rare plants. In 1762 he purchased the Upton Hall estate in East London, building a rock garden to grow alpines such as *Ranunculus glacialis* from the Swiss Alps and the sky-blue *Gentiana bavarica*.

JOHN FOTHERGILL.MD.FRS.SA..

Dr John Fothergill. Mezzotint by
V. Green, 1781, after Gilbert Stuart.
(Wellcome Collection)

In 1775 Fothergill and Scottish physician Dr William Pitcairn commissioned Thomas Blaikie, a young gardener from Edinburgh 'to undertake a journey to the Alps and Switzerland in search of rare and curious plants'. Blaikie kept a detailed diary of his trip and returned with 447 different species for his sponsors. Fothergill commissioned several famous artists, including George Ehret and John Miller, to record his plants. After his death, Catherine the Great purchased the painting collection and had them sent to Russia where they remain in the Komarov Botanical Library in St Petersburg.

Fothergill's contemporary John Blackburne (1693–1786) created a remarkable garden at Orford Hall near Warrington in Lancashire. It was known for his 'pine stove', which was one of the first in England to produce ripe pineapples. In April 1767 he wrote to William Logan in Pennsylvania that he was 'going to make a piece of rock work for plants that grow in rocks, viz: sedum, stonecrop, licopodiums, lychens, mosses, etc; most likely your part of America affords many pretty sorts of these, which as we have not many of these, would be very acceptable'. Blackburne's daughter, Anna, herself a noted naturalist, boasted to Carl Linnaeus in 1771 that her father had one of the best plant collections in the country. The Welsh naturalist and traveller Thomas Pennant visited Orford Hall, admiring Blackburne's 'rock plants on artificial rocks'.

Chelsea Physic Garden, founded in 1673 by the Worshipful Society of Apothecaries, was originally situated at Westminster but was moved to Chelsea in 1676. The pond rockery

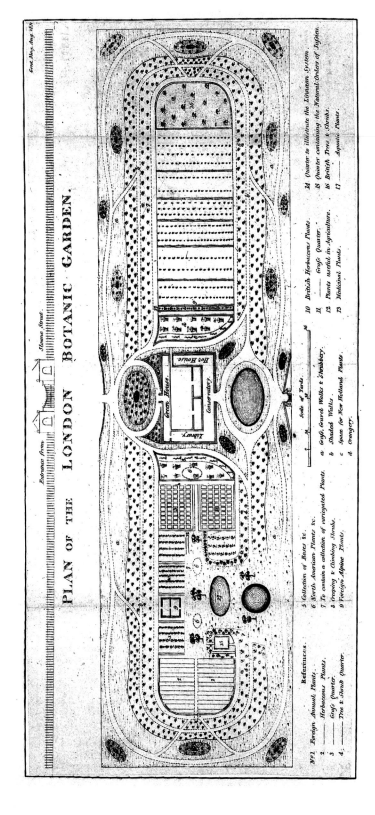

Plan of the botanic garden at Chelsea in 1810.

9

in the centre of the garden is probably the oldest surviving rock garden in the United Kingdom. In September 1772 head gardener Stanesby Alchorne (1727–1800) purchased 40 tonnes of masonry stones from the Tower of London, which was undergoing alterations. He had these laid at the garden, at his own expense, 'for the Purpose of raising an Artificial Rock to cultivate plants which delight in such soil'. This stone became part of an eclectic mixture of reused materials, including chunks of brick from a Chelsea kiln, large quantities of flint and chalk donated by John Chandler and lumps of basalt brought as ship's ballast from Iceland by Sir Joseph Banks (1743–1820) on his return from the Hekla volcano, known by the Norse people as 'the Gateway to Hell'.

The rock garden is roughly circular in shape and was constructed around what remained of a lily pond built by John Evelyn in 1685. In 1946 Bill Mackenzie rebuilt the rock garden, explaining to Graham Stuart Thomas that the contrast between the white Portland stone from the Tower and the black basaltic lava was 'too much of a contrast to live with'. The pond is home to a giant clam shell, one of many specimens brought back by Banks from his voyage to Tahiti with Captain Cook on the *Endeavour*. Banks had grown up at Revesby Abbey in Lincolnshire where he developed his love of the natural world. In 1766 he joined HMS *Niger* as ship's botanist, under the command of Sir Thomas Adams, to survey the coast of Newfoundland and Labrador. Banks collected many previously unrecorded species of plants and animals. He was generous in his support of other scientists, making his extensive collections of plants and books open to anyone who asked, but was an unapologetic supporter of slavery, which he thought was essential to the economic power of the British Empire.

The beauty of the Alpine mountains inspired many people to create alpine gardens. (Image by tizman supreme/Pixabay)

The Schönbrunn Palace in Vienna, Austria, was the main summer residence of the Habsburg rulers. In 1803 archdukes Johann, Rainer and Anton created an alpine garden there. Johann in particular was known for his love of the Austrian Alps and would travel to the mountains to escape court life. He had a traditional alpine farmhouse erected in the park and employed a herdsman wearing regional costume to care for the imperial cattle and blow his alpenhorn. The alpine garden was transferred to the grounds of the Belvedere palaces in 1865. The Austrian botanist Anton Kerner von Marilaun (1831–98) conducted many experiments to investigate plant adaptations in mountain species and cultivated specimens at different altitudes so that he could observe any changes occurring in subsequent generations. He established an experimental garden on the Blaser Mountain, in the Tyrol. His book *Die Cultur der Alpenpflanzen* (1864), based on his ecological studies of alpines, encouraged gardeners to simulate the natural growing conditions of mountain plants.

One of the most influential horticultural writers was William Robinson (1838–1935). In 1862 he was put in charge of the educational and herbaceous department of the Royal Botanic Society in Regent's Park. He started to write articles for *The Gardeners' Chronicle* and in 1866 resigned his post to devote himself to travelling and horticultural writing. Robinson's *Alpine Flowers for the English Garden* (1870) aimed 'to dispel a very general error, that the exquisite flowers of alpine countries cannot be grown in gardens'. It was instrumental in a surge of interest in rock garden plants in the United Kingdom. He

Snowdrops growing in grass in the Greek Rhodope mountains.

encouraged planting alpines in properly constructed rock gardens and suggested the naturalising of swathes of bulbs in grass. His weekly magazine *The Garden* advocated for a natural style of gardening rather than the carpet bedding displays then popular. Robinson was a friend of Gertrude Jekyll and helped plan her garden at Munstead Wood where she had her own rock garden.

Like Robinson, Henry Correvon (1854–1939) did much to promote the cultivation of alpine plants. Born at Yverdon in Switzerland, Correvon was sent first to Geneva, then to Germany and France to learn the horticultural trade. When he returned, he found the family business suffering from neglect and set to work to rebuild it. In 1877 he exhibited a collection of alpines that he had grown from seed but in July that year the nursery was almost destroyed by a cyclone. The stocks of low-growing alpine plants had managed to survive and prompted Correvon to specialise in plants for rock gardens. Correvon's *Les Plantes des Alpes* was published in France in 1884. In 1902 he bought a vineyard at Chêne-Bourg which he developed as a demonstration garden with limestone rocks brought from the Salève and granite from the Alps.

Correvon's Floraire Nursery became famous throughout Europe. The Norman Tower rock garden at Windsor Castle, created by Sir Dighton Probyn from Norfolk carrstone, was stocked with plants supplied by Floraire, said to have been much enjoyed by King Edward VII and his wife, Alexandra. The botanist Alphonso do Candollo persuaded Correvon to learn English and in 1886 he travelled to England and wrote about the gardens he visited, including Ellen Willmott's rock garden at Warley Place. At the age of seventy-three he went on a speaking tour of America to promote alpine gardening. Correvon credited Ida Agassiz Higginson as being the first in the United States to successfully grow alpine rhododendrons, gentians and edelweiss. Sunset Hill in Manchester, Massachusetts, the garden created by Ida and her husband Henry Lee Higginson, was described as the finest alpine garden in America.

Gentian with candytufts. (Image by Wollzimmer/Pixabay)

Join the Club

Whilst gardening can seem a solitary activity, many gardeners value the benefits of joining a garden society. These include meeting people with a shared passion, swapping seeds and plants and attending shows and garden visits. Rock garden enthusiasts can be found across the world. In Switzerland the Association Pour la Protection des Plantes, founded by Correvon with an emphasis on conservation, had attracted 200 members by June 1884. The Vancouver Island Rock and Alpine Garden Society had their first meeting in 1921 and held their first flower show in 1939. The Schynige Platte Alpine Garden Society, based in the Bernese Oberland region of Switzerland, was created in 1927 and two years later opened the Schynige Platte display gardens to the public.

Belden Saur, Carl Krippendorf and Robert Senior, a recognised authority on the genus *Campanula,* formed the Rock Garden Society of Ohio in 1929, attracting members from all over the United States and Europe. Regulations stipulated that the applicant's garden had to be approved by the membership. There was no such requirement in the United Kingdom when in the same year the Alpine Garden Society (AGS) was formed at the suggestion of Sir William Lawrence. The AGS is one of the world's largest specialist plant societies. It aims to promote an interest in all aspects of alpine plants, their cultivation in rock gardens and plant conservation in natural habitats. Its headquarters at Pershore in Worcestershire has a demonstration alpine garden, alpine house and library on site. A highly regarded journal is produced and lectures and conferences are organised.

Alpine plants at the Royal Horticultural Society's London Show, 2010.

The AGS has close links with the Scottish Rock Garden Club (SRGC), which was founded in Edinburgh in 1933. Local groups help organise plant shows across Scotland as well as talks and other events. The club has operated a members' seed exchange since 1948. The SRGC website has a huge range of resources including back issues of the twice-yearly journal which are freely shared with all. There is a very active online forum which connects people around the world, allowing them to share images of their own gardens and plants seen on their travels. There are similar clubs run in the Netherlands and Belgium.

The North American Rock Garden Society was founded in 1934 as the American Rock Garden Society. The American alpine plant the shooting star, *Dodecatheon*, was chosen as the society's symbol. The society shared its aims with those in Britain. Founder member Martha Houghton travelled to England in the spring of 1936 to attend the first AGS conference and visit many alpine gardens. The society now has forty chapters across the United States and Canada. The first Year Book was published in 1937. A high-quality illustrated journal, *The Rock Garden Quarterly*, is also produced.

Alpine gardening is also very popular in the Czech Republic and the Rock Gardeners Club Prague (KSP) was formed in 1970 with the inaugural meeting held in a concert hall on Slovanský Ostrov. Many Czech growers have innovative approaches to rock garden design and the society organises international conferences which are very well attended. A society display garden is cared for in the garden of the Baroque Church of St John of Nepomuk on the Rock.

Dodecatheon pulchellum, the dark-throat shooting star.

Rock Gardens on Show

The first World's Fair took place in Prague (in the modern-day Czech Republic) in 1791 to celebrate the coronation of Leopold II as King of Bohemia. In London, the Great Exhibition of 1851 was held in Paxton's Crystal Palace in Hyde Park. The Ideal Home Exhibition, founded in 1908 by the *Daily Mail*, primarily as a way of increasing advertising revenue, also stimulated debate about housing conditions, child welfare and, after the war, 'homes fit for heroes'. It was held at the Olympia Exhibition Centre in London until 1978, when it moved to Earls Court. These large-scale exhibitions frequently presented the latest trends in horticulture. In the United States, the 1933 Century of Progress fair in Chicago was organised to celebrate the city's centennial. Despite being held in the midst of the Great Depression, 39 million visitors paid to view exhibits which included an old mill garden with swans in the millpond, a recreation of a Belgian village and an alpine rock garden.

The Royal Horticultural Society (RHS) has held flower shows since 1833. In the 1890s miniature rock gardens began to be seen as exhibits in the marquee. Their Great Spring Show was first held at Chelsea in May 1913. There were seventeen show gardens exhibited that year. The only gold-medal winner was the rock garden created by John Wood, an alpine garden specialist from Boston Spa. Clarence Elliott, who had a nursery specialising in alpine plants at Six Hills near Stevenage, joked that Wood's garden was so realistic it just needed some alpine goats. The following year Wood duly added a pair of goats to his display. Large rock gardens created by firms such as Backhouse of York, James Pulham and Son and the Ingwersens of Birch Farm Nursery, East Grinstead, dominated the show gardens at Chelsea until the 1950s.

THE DELL ROCK GARDEN. *(By WALLACE)*
'DAILY MAIL' IDEAL HOME EXHIBITION, 1930

Demonstration rock garden at the Ideal Home Exhibition, 1930.

©1933. R H D CO.   ALPINE GARDEN

The Chicago: A Century of Progress exhibition of 1933 included an alpine garden. (Official postcard of A Century of Progress, The Reuben H. Donnelley Corporation)

Since the 1920s the AGS has organised regular competitive plant shows all over the UK. The Joint Rock Garden Plant Committee was formed in 1936 to consider plants with potential for garden use or exhibition for awards. The committee is made up of members of the RHS, the AGS and the SRGC. It tends to be male-dominated, although the renowned photographer and alpine gardener Valerie Finnis was a member for twenty years, from 1962 to 1982. Exhibits are grown to high standards and include plants rarely seen elsewhere. Avid competitors often travel great distances to show their plants. Not everyone is enthusiastic though and in 2015 garden writer Noel Kingsbury commented on a 'kind of unnatural perfection' and worried about the 'competitive element which brought out an odd kind of underlying nastiness which is generally rare in the garden world'.

Right: *Iris afghanica* exhibited at the Royal Horticultural Society's London Show in 2010.

Below: The East Anglian Show of the Alpine Garden Society, May 2010.

2

Rock Art and Craft

Rock art predates written history. Many archaeologists are reluctant to use the term art to describe carvings such as the cup and ring motifs on stone found across the Atlantic seaboard of Europe and in the Mediterranean. Nobody really knows if they were created as art, for religious ritual, to mark territory or simply as a game to keep the children occupied. Similar forms are found throughout the world and can date back at least 8,000 years. Ancient rock paintings have survived only in sheltered sites, particularly caves, but allow us poignant glimpses of the lives of people who lived before us. The use of stone for monuments is also ancient. Tales in the Bible relate that Samuel erected a stone he named Ebenezer (stone of help) to commemorate a victory against the Philistines. Jacob set up a stone pillar to mark the place he had heard God speak, anointing it with wine and oil. The king of Judah (*c.* 640–609 BC) abolished the practice of erecting stelae because some people attached religious significance to the stones themselves, which he considered idolatrous.

Ancient cup and ring motifs carved on stone at Roughting Linn in Northumberland.

Certainly, many people can feel an emotional attachment to a stone. This may manifest simply in taking home a pleasing pebble as a reminder of a day spent stone skipping on a lake. In *Stone Will Answer* (2023) the stone mason Beatrice Searle described her more arduous trek through the Norwegian mountains carrying a 40-kg rock on which she had carved her footprints. She was inspired by the Ladykirk Stone of St Mary's Church in South Ronaldsay. In northern Europe footprints carved in stone are associated with the inauguration of kings. The new king would stand in the footprints, demonstrating his connection with the land and testifying to his intention to follow in the footsteps of his ancestors.

In the Diquís Delta of Costa Rica there are over 300 mysterious stone spheres whose production and meaning are unknown. Unlike those at Rock City in Kansas and the Moeraki Boulders cluster in New Zealand, these pre-Columbian artefacts are not naturally occurring concretions, but are man-made and distinctive in their size and perfection. More famous of course is the dramatic stone circle on Salisbury Plain in England. Stonehenge, erected in the late Neolithic period, around 2500 BC, is a Scheduled Ancient Monument. Its stones are protected and cannot be taken away for rock garden use but certainly have inspired gardeners. Henry Herbert, the Earl of Pembroke, had a miniature model of Stonehenge created in the gardens of Wilton House in Wiltshire. It was praised by the

In southern Spain there are a number of carved rocks that are thought to have been used for sky burials.

The purpose of the stone circle at Stonehenge on Salisbury Plain is still debated by archaeologists.

antiquarian William Stukeley in 1743 but has not survived. In the Regency period Major Richard West had a half-scale version built to admire from his home Quinta House at Oswestry. Scottish horticulturalist John Loudon described a garden structure based on Stonehenge at Alton Towers, Staffordshire, in 1826. This remains today but actually bears little resemblance to the Salisbury stones.

Stonehenge itself has attracted garden lovers. The Salisbury Plain Dahlia Society took flowers to Stonehenge when they staged flower shows at the site between 1842 and 1845. These were attended by between 5,000 and 10,000 people each year. A special exhibition held at the Stonehenge visitor centre in September 2023 gave modern visitors the chance to admire the 5,000 dahlias in a display that including large sculptures created by local flower-arranging groups. Such celebrations demonstrate how people continue to enjoy interactions with ancient stones.

Rock Garden Design – Fashion and Trends

A love of the natural wonders that surround us is a common human trait, so it is unsurprising that many gardeners enjoy combining stone and plants. In the eighteenth century, garden features were designed not merely as objects of beauty but also as stimuli for the intellect and emotion. Rococo gardens made extensive use of rocks, pebblework and shells to decorate follies and grottos. Grottos were inspired by the natural caves and rocky shelters used by humans since antiquity. Those could stimulate philosophical discussions

The hermit's cave at Batsford Arboretum, created for Algernon Bertram Freeman-Mitford in the late nineteenth century.

about journeys to the mysterious depths of the earth. The poet and satirist Alexander Pope (1688–1744) had seen the grottos of Palazzo Pitti in Florence during a visit to Italy and created an elaborate grotto under his Twickenham villa. He diverted a natural spring to run along the floor and water dripped from the roof through mosses. Pope was fascinated by rocks and gemstones and friends supplied him with rare specimens for his grotto. The physician and naturalist Hans Sloane sent him rock from the Giant's Causeway in Ireland. Mirrors and glass were used to reflect the view of the river. In 1725 Pope wrote in a letter that when the grotto was lit up with lamps, 'a thousand pointed rays glitter'.

The extraordinary Sanspareil Rock Garden in the German town of Bayreuth was commissioned in the mid-eighteenth century by Frederick, Margrave of Brandenburg-Bayreuth, and his wife, the Margravine Wilhelmine, also known as Princess Friederike Sophie Wilhelmine of Prussia. Wilhelmine was the much-loved older sister of Frederick the Great. The beech forest around Zwernitz Castle had been used as a hunting chase since medieval times. Located in the Franconian Jura mountains, it was dominated by many bizarre natural rock formations. In 1744 work began to create a 'garden of wonders'. Garden designers, the French architect Joseph Saint-Pierre, who worked on the opera house in Bayreuth, and the sculptor Giovanni Battista Pedrozzi were employed, but in a letter to her brother, Wilhelmine declared that 'Nature herself was the architect'. Wilhelmine was an intelligent and cultured woman and was fascinated by the French novel *The Adventures of Telemachus* (1699) by François Fénelon, which told the imaginary adventures of the son of Odysseus.

The setting for the novel was the island of Ogygia, home of the nymph Calypso. Wilhelmine had her garden created as a fantasy world using natural rock formations as a backdrop to grottos, temples and an amphitheatre inspired by the story. Saint-Pierre based his design for the amphitheatre on a stone theatre on the Hellbrunner Berg, near Salzburg. When a lady of the court first saw the garden in 1746 she exclaimed, '*Ah, c'est sans pareil!*' ('It has no equal!'). Margrave Friedrich was so taken by the phrase that he had Zwernitz renamed Sanspareil. Garden building on a grand scale is expensive and some of Wilhelmine's plans had to be curtailed. After her death the Aeolus Tower was destroyed

Left: The garden at Sanspareil. (Image by Wolfgang Eckert, Pixabay)

Below: Engraving of the garden at Sansparail.

Die Aeolusgrotte zu Sansparcil.

in a thunderstorm and the gardens were closed and fell into disrepair. Restoration work began in 1951 and the gardens are now open to the public.

The politician Thomas Whately (1726 –72) published *Observations on Modern Gardening* in 1770. He considered that use of rocks required great thought in their selection, writing, 'their most distinguished characters are, dignity, terror, and fancy: the expressions of all are constantly wild; and sometimes a rocky scene is only wild, without pretensions to any particular character'. Horace Walpole (1717–97) had done a grand tour of France, Switzerland and Italy. He was unimpressed by Baroque gardens such as Versailles, which he felt symbolised the oppression of nature. Commenting ironically on French architect René Louis Girardin's 1777 essay on landscaping, he said:

Mon. Girardin, being a rigid classic, will tolerate nothing but Grecian Temples and domes ... His receipt for making rocks in your garden is not less admirable: 'Take a mountain, break it into pieces with a hammer, number the fragments and observe their antecedent positions: place them in their original order, cover the junctures with mould: plant ivy and grass and weeds, which will hide the fractures, and so you may have a cart-load of Snowdon or Penmenmaur in the middle of your bowling-green, and no soul will suspect that it did not grow there.

Jane Loudon in *Gardening for Ladies* (1845) seemed less averse to the idea of a rockery in the lawn:

Where there are collections of such plants as Saxifrages or other alpines, or of Cistuses, Helianthemums, or other mountain shrubs, rockwork is very desirable; and in such cases it may be placed on a lawn, as a feature in a general collection of herbaceous plants or shrubs arranged according to the natural system; but rockwork as an ornamental object, or as a nidus [nook] for a miscellaneous collection of plants, should always be in an open airy situation, near a pond, or surrounded by a walk.

An article in *The Gardener's Magazine* of 1831 proclaimed that 'few objects produce a more striking effect than immense masses of stone, piled together in such a way as at once to give a particular character of rocky mass, and to form a proper nidus for plants'. Joseph Paxton, writing in 1841, disagreed, calling the trend for piles of rocks on a lawn 'one of the most monstrous infringements on taste'. He believed that 'seclusion is indispensable for rockeries and they do not mix and combine harmoniously with other features of a pleasure-garden. No subject in the gardening profession calls for a more vigorous exercise of skill and talent than the formation of rockeries and their appendages'.

The American Robert B. Cridland, whose *Practical Landscape Gardening* (1916) was aimed at suburban home owners, included a chapter on rockwork discussing those composed of natural stones as well as artificial stalactites and 'picturesque designs'. He had strong views on the rock gardens in the United States, saying:

The making of rockwork has been but very little practiced in this country, and is often undertaken by men of but little taste and less experience. This will account for the many ridiculous and tasteless specimens of the work, to be met with in different parts of the country, and which have caused many men of true taste to condemn the whole art.

A rock garden displayed at the Cincinnati Horticultural Society exhibition of 1854 by G. M. Kern certainly attracted a good deal of opprobrium. Edouard André, landscape architect for Sefton Park in Liverpool and the Villa Borghese gardens in Rome, used it in his book *Traité général de la composition des parcs et jardins* (1879) as an example of what he called '*Le Musee des horreurs*'. It featured a mock rocky mountain, surmounted with a model castle, at the foot of which was a small circular pond with two mermen blowing 'what appears to be peppermint candy out of ear trumpets'. The pool was surrounded by alpine and woodland plants and 'is garnished on either side by seven of those small nondescript combinations of pine shavings and green paint which do duty as trees in children's German toy sets and a very old broom, set handle downward, completes the edifice. The lake is appropriately margined by cobble stones, alternated by turnips in a luxuriant state of vegetation'.

It is perhaps unsurprising that Joseph Breck of Massachusetts recommended in 1851 that the rockery should be concealed from the 'general flower-garden'. He advised that rock gardens should be shaded for the benefit of the plants. This consideration of plant requirements was obviously essential for those wanting a varied collection of plants. George William Johnson's *Dictionary of Modern Gardening* of 1847 recommended that it should be plants that are the focus of any rockwork. The *Gardener's Magazine* of 1831 reported that at Hoole House the rockwork was 'so generally covered with creeping and alpine plants, that it all mingles together in one mass'. Indeed, some rock plants can be somewhat over-vigorous. Beverley Nichols in *Down the Garden Path* (1932) warned:

Having obtained your design, and buried your rocks, your next task is to exercise phenomenal restraint about the things which you put in. I have always been a fervent advocate of birth-control, but since I have been the owner of a rock garden my fervour has increased a hundred-fold. The prolificacy of the common saxifrage is positively embarrassing. The speed with which the rock rose reproduces itself brings a blush to the cheek. Violas appear to have absolutely no self-control, and as for the alyssum … well, if we behaved like the alyssum, Australia would be over-populated before the year is out.

Alpine Wall Gardens

In her 1899 book *Wood and Garden*, Gertrude Jekyll suggested a loose wall as 'one of the best and simplest ways of growing rock plants'. Henry Correvon agreed and the following year wrote an article, 'Wall Gardens', for *The Garden* magazine. Photographs taken by Ellen Willmott showed a wall at his Geneva nursery in which grew rosettes of saxifrages and other alpine plants. Jekyll developed her ideas in *Wall and Water Gardens* (1901) based on observations of plants growing in dry-stone walls in England and abroad. In many of the gardens she designed with Edwin Lutyens retaining walls were perforated with gaps, allowing cascades of *Erigeron karvinskianus*, aubrieta or rock pinks to soften the hard landscaping. The Royal Botanic Garden at Edinburgh had a similar red sandstone wall, which in 1934 was home to *Ramonda pyrenaica*, *Primula forrestii* and Californian lewisias.

When Margery and Walter Fish moved to East Lambrook Manor in Somerset they started to create the garden described in Margery's book *We Made a Garden* (1956). The book is not just a guide to gardening but also a picture of a marriage and a warning of the difficulties of sharing a garden when two people have very different gardening styles. Walter liked big and bold summer flowering flowers such as delphiniums and dahlias. Margery preferred snowdrops, hellebores and small alpine plants. She was pleased when he suggested she build a rock garden but found it was only because 'he wanted some way of disposing of the bigger rubbish that couldn't be buried. So all the oil stoves, bits of bedsteads, lumps of iron and rolls of wire netting were distributed against the walls and the rest of the job was handed over to me'. Making the best of things, Margery covered all the rubbish and went through heaps of stones, selecting the nicest looking ones to build a rockery.

Plants in the wild that colonise cliff faces, such as these saxifrages in Greece, provide inspiration for alpine walls.

A drystone wall in Northumberland.

25

A wall planted with alpine plants including lewisias at John Massey's Ashwood Nursery.

Margery reports that she was pleased with her efforts until a visitor gently explained that it was a disaster. The stones were laid at the wrong angle and so in heavy rain most of the soil would be washed away. Fortunately, she had a cousin who re-laid the stones for her 'to give the effect of level strata of outcrop, something I would never of dreamed of and I've never ceased to admire'. Margery herself built terraces of dry-stone walls and tucked alpine plants into the crevices. The first wall she made met with husbandly approval, but she reported, 'he was less enthusiastic as time went on as he thought I was spending too much time poking "belly-crawlers into rat-holes" instead of doing jobs he thought more important.' Those 'belly-crawlers' have outlived both Walter and Margery and the garden continues to open to the public each year, starting with the snowdrops in February.

Tufa is a soft form of limestone deposited as calcium carbonate-rich groundwater is exposed to the atmosphere. It is common in many parts of the world and was used as a lightweight building material in Roman times. Tufa is porous and can absorb a lot of water, releasing this slowly during drier periods. The ability of plant roots to penetrate into tufa makes it an ideal substrate for many otherwise difficult to grow alpines. A wall made out of concrete and tufa was created in 1968 at the botanical garden of Mendel University in Brno in the Czech Republic under the guidance of the rock garden curator Josef Holzbecher. He

Above left: Snowdrops flowering at East Lambrook Manor.

Above right: Saxifrages growing in a tufa wall at Harlow Carr garden in Harrogate, North Yorkshire.

used many different materials including metal, concrete, stone and wood to create a variety of plant habitats in the garden. These inspired other Czech rock gardeners to develop tufa walls and towers as garden features that have been imitated by other enthusiasts around the world.

Artificial Rocks

The diarist John Evelyn (1620–1706) in his *Elysium Britannicum* advised his readers on how to build a mountain in their garden. He suggested that if natural rock was unavailable then 'the defect thereoff may be well supplied by Rocks made artificially'. Artificial rock has a long history. In the Roman city of Pozzuoli, near Naples, it was found that the local volcanic sand, pozzolana, reacted chemically with water, forming the basis for the first effective concrete. This made possible the construction of the massive domed ceiling of the Pantheon in Rome. In England, the Lambeth manufacturer Richard Holt published in 1730, *A short treatise of artificial stone, as 'tis now made, and converted into all manner of curious embellishments and proper ornaments of architecture*. It discussed how by the use of artificial stone, the ancients have 'most ingeniously prevented all the mischiefs of Time itself'. He boasted that his own recipe was stronger than the best natural stone.

27

In the late eighteenth century industry was dominated by men, but Eleanor Coade (1733–1821), the daughter of a wool merchant, worked first as a linen draper, then produced her own brand of stone. She joined Daniel Pincot, a stone maker who is thought to have taken over Richard Holt's Lambeth business. Coade stone was widely used in the best gardens of the day, mostly for commemorative monuments and garden ornaments such as the River God at Ham House, near Richmond in Surrey. In this work, priced at 100 guineas in the 1784 Coade catalogue, the reclining personification of Father Thames is shown on a Coade stone rock.

The best-known artificial stone for rock gardens is Pulhamite, a patented modified rock developed in the 1840s by James Pulham (1820–98) from Woodbridge in Suffolk and marketed as Pulham's Portland Stone Cement. Pulham was succeeded by his son and then by three further generations of eldest sons, all named James. Pulhamite was applied to a masonry core or backing structure to produce textures and colour variations mimicking natural rock. Pulham described his methods in his illustrated publication *Picturesque Ferneries and Rock Garden Scenery* (1877). The firm constructed a large number of rock gardens, follies and grottoes using a combination of any naturally occurring stone and Pulhamite. It won medals at London's Great Exhibition of 1851 and was granted a Royal Warrant in 1895 by the Prince of Wales. The rockeries by the lake at Sandringham House in Norfolk survive today.

Battersea Park was built on land formerly used for market gardens, growing crops such as lavender and asparagus. The park was laid out by architect Sir James Pennethorne and James Robert Pulham was commissioned in 1871 to construct 'Waterfalls, Rocky stream, [and a] Cave for shady seat on the peninsula and in other parts of the Park'. It was the first example of his work in a London park. A waterfall known as The Cascades was fed

Leonardslee, West Sussex, May 2009. (Image by Adrian Herridge)

by water from the pump house. A smaller rock feature to the west is called The Owlery. The waterfalls have not been running since the 1980s, although even in 1900 the weekly illustrated newspaper *The Graphic* reported that visitors were sometimes disappointed to find them dry.

One of the largest of Pulham's commissions was the rock garden at Leonardslee in East Sussex. It was owned by Sir Edmund Loder (1849–1920). His obituary by Herbert Maxwell recorded that Loder was 'possessed of ample means and abundant leisure'. He devoted much of his early life to travel and shooting. 'In the pursuit of big game in four continents his fine marksmanship enabled him to make the very large collection of horned and other trophies now preserved at Leonardslee. He was among the last of British sportsmen to take toll of the dwindling herds of bison in North-west America.' When not taking toll of dwindling herds, Loder was a keen gardener. On purchasing the Leonardslee estate in 1889 he filled the grounds with exotic plants and animals. The Pulhams were brought in to create the extensive rock garden near the house. It was planted up with a spectacular mixture of azaleas, small conifers and herbaceous plants. They used a mixture of natural and artificial sandstone to build a mound containing artificial caves for Loder's mouflon. These are now used as breeding pens for the wallabies who live on the estate.

The seaside town of Ramsgate in Kent has been popular since the 1820s when the then Princess Victoria made several visits. In 1884 the borough council started to improve the road system and the coastal frontage to increase the town's appeal as a holiday destination. A road from the harbour to the East Cliff was constructed by the Pulham firm to make it look as if the road cut through a steep gorge, with rocky cliffs on either side. Pulhamite rocks were used to shore up the banks of the gorge and a cascade was created halfway up.

The Pulham rock garden at Ramsgate.

It was considered such a success that the Pulhams were commissioned to build the 'Sun Palace' rock garden at the Winterstoke and Courtstairs Chine, an ornamental walkway from the cliff top to the undercliff promenade. The Ramsgate Pulhamite constructions are still popular with tourists and were listed on the National Heritage List for England in 1988.

Bawdsey Manor was built at the mouth of the River Deben in Suffolk in 1886 and enlarged in 1895 by Sir William Cuthbert Quilter, who was a stockbroker and art collector. He commissioned the Pulhams to create a number of features including a round garden on the site of an old Martello tower and a water garden which was cared for by Harry Thrower, the father of the broadcaster and gardener Percy Thrower. The manor is situated on a cliff top, and a Pulhamite artificial cliff 110 metre long and up to 10 metres high was built with a path running along its length. The manor is now used by PGL for activity courses and children's holidays.

The cliff face at Bawdsey Manor is the work of the Pulham firm.

3

Rolling Stones

The English essayist and historian Edward Gibbon (1737–94) remarked that 'foreign travel completes the education of an English gentleman'. It is of course not only gentlemen who benefit from travelling. The first recorded female pilgrim, the fourth-century traveller Egeria, wrote about her travels through Europe and the East in search of places featured in the Bible. In the fourteenth century when Geoffrey Chaucer wrote *The Canterbury Tales* his 'worthy woman from Bath' had travelled to Jerusalem three times, visited Rome, Boulogne and Cologne and had seen 'many strange rivers'. Mary Shelley visited the Mer de Glace glacier in the French Alps in 1817 and her impressions made their way into her novel *Frankenstein*: 'I remained in a recess of rock, gazing at this wonderful and stupendous scene. The sea, or rather the vast river of ice, wound among its dependent mountains, whose

Carl Spitzweg's *English Tourists in Campagna*, 1835. (Berlin State Museums)

The tourist may see plants, such as this doronicum on Mount Parnassus in Greece.

aerial summits hung over its recesses. Their icy glittering peaks shone in the sunlight over the clouds. My heart, which was before sorrowful, now swelled with something like joy.'

The grand tour of the seventeenth to nineteenth centuries, however, was principally seen as a mobile finishing school for wealthy young men. The tour was an extended trip through Europe, with Italy as a key destination and aimed to show the cultural and natural wonders of Europe and instil a love of art, history and language. The famous architect Inigo Jones was accompanied on his tour of Italy in 1613–14 by his patron Thomas Howard, 14th Earl of Arundel. He visited cities including Naples, Parma, Venice and Rome returning with impressions of Italian architecture that infused his subsequent work. When the artist Joseph Wright of Derby travelled through Italy in the mid-1770s he was profoundly influenced by the landscapes, particularly the volcanos, caverns and grottos that he encountered. The paintings that he made from his travel sketches, especially those which show the dramatic chiaroscuro light effects for which Wright is renowned, are some of his best loved works. They were certainly those he most enjoyed creating. On his return to England he wrote to a friend, 'I know not how it is, tho' I am engaged in portraits ... I find myself continually stealing off, and getting to Landscapes'.

Those fortunate enough to have enjoyed a grand tour would usually return with more than just memories of foreign countries and the associated life experiences. Tangible souvenirs included crates full of books, scientific instruments, works of art and interesting artefacts to be displayed back home. In a trend akin to the 'selfies' of today's generation, tourists of the young social elite often sat for a portrait whilst on their travels as a visual demonstration of their culture and sophistication. For those interested in horticulture, a tour of Europe opened up the opportunity to study new flora, to explore how they were used in gardens

Grotto in the Gulf of Salerno by Joseph Wright of Derby (1774).

and to bring back sculpture and plants for their own gardens. Alpine plants seen in the mountains inspired many to try to grow them. Shropshire-born Thomas Johnes (1748–1816) undertook a grand tour that included France, Spain, Switzerland and Italy, returning in 1771. When Johnes inherited Hafod Uchtryd in Ceredigion on his father's death in 1780, he and his second wife, Jane, had a new mansion built in the Gothic style and landscaped the surrounding estate along picturesque principles to embellish its natural beauty.

Their first child, Mariamne, was born in June 1784 and showed an early interest in botany. The family were friends with Sir James Edward Smith of Norwich, an English botanist and founder of the Linnean Society. Both father and daughter regularly wrote to him. Mariamne reported finding a maidenhead fern and offered to send it to Smith. He was impressed by her enthusiasm and knowledge and that she had nearly memorised his book *English Botany*. Her proud father reported: 'I only shine in Botany but like the Moon by borrowed light, or rather to please her, who is dearer to me than the light.' In 1795 Johnes asked Scottish agriculturalist James Anderson to design a garden for his daughter where she could look after her growing collection of plants. She particularly favoured small alpine species. Anderson chose a south-facing precipice as the site for Mariamne's garden, accessed by a narrow craggy path and created a secret retreat with views out across the landscape. It was described in 1803 as 'not so studiously ornamental' as her mother's gardens but it 'exhibits in a nursed state many of the most curious plants, which are the natural growth of high exposures in foreign climates'.

In March 1807 the house at Hafod caught fire and burnt to the ground. The family spent most of the next four years in London while the house was rebuilt. Mariamne

33

had been ill for much of her childhood and sadly died, just before her twenty-seventh birthday. Her grief-sticken parents had her buried back at Hafod and commissioned the renowned sculptor Francis Chantrey to produce a marble monument for Hafod church. The Hafod estate went through long periods of neglect but is now in the care of the National Trust.

John Claudius Loudon (1783–1843), the Scottish landscape gardener and horticultural writer, spent a year travelling through Russia, Poland, Germany and Sweden from 1813. He used the opportunity to visit as many gardens as possible. A second trip starting from Paris in May 1819 included Lyons, Marseilles and Nice, before he sailed to Genoa from where he explored Italy, including Pompeii and Herculaneum. His friend Sir Joseph Banks provided letters of introduction to many botanists and horticulturalists enabling Loudon to collect materials for his *Encyclopedia of Gardening*, which he published in 1822.

Loudon was hired by Charles Talbot, 15th Earl of Shrewsbury (1753–1827) to develop the gardens at Alton Towers, although he reported sardonically: 'though he consulted almost every artist, ourselves among the rest, he seems only to have done so for the purpose of avoiding whatever an artist might recommend'. Lord Shrewsbury and his wife had moved to Alton in Staffordshire in 1814 and set to work to create a home surrounded by one of the largest formal gardens in Britain, employing hundreds of engineers, craftsmen and labourers. It was a site of spectacular natural beauty. Loudon wrote, 'the natural character of this part of the country is grand and picturesque, with a solitary and wild air, approaching to the savage'. He was less impressed with what the Earl achieved there, saying that the design had been carried out 'with much more fancy than sound judgment'.

The rock garden at Alton Towers.

Describing the valley garden, Loudon reported:

As the sandstone rock protrudes from the sides of the valley in immense masses, abundance of use has been made of it to form caves, caverns, and covered seats; it has even been carved into figures, and we have Indian temples excavated in it, covered with hieroglyphics, and in one place a projecting rock is formed into a huge serpent, with a spear-shaped iron tongue and glass eyes.

The garden had cascading waterfalls, hidden walkways and an imitation Stonehenge. A replica Swiss Cottage housed a Welsh harpist who played for garden visitors. The garden provided employment for many local women who were kept busy weeding, deadheading flowers and tidying up. On special occasions the women dressed in Swiss costumes to increase the 'alpine' impression.

The 6th Duke of Devonshire, William George Spencer Cavendish, was a somewhat eccentric man who loved jokes and kept a log of the weights of all of his guests, recording that on 7 December 1816 the Grand Duke Nicholas (later Tsar of Russia) weighed 13 stone 7 pounds, the same as the duke himself. Cavendish was a keen horticulturalist and President of the Royal Horticultural Society for over twenty years. He met the young Joseph Paxton at Chiswick House Gardens and offered him the post of head gardener at Chatsworth. In 1838 Paxton accompanied the duke on a grand tour. Their journey through the Alps was a particular highlight, and on their return, Paxton built the duke a monumental rock garden as a reminder of that time, aiming for an 'imitation of the natural features of a wild and rugged scene'. He was determined that rock should be the focus, with plants taking a secondary role. The garden used locally quarried gritstone rocks and Paxton designed a steam-powered machine to lift them into position. Paths were laid to wind between passes of tightly packed rock. Below the main rock garden, he built an imitation of the Strid at Bolton Abbey, the duke's North Yorkshire estate, where the River Wharfe forces through a narrow gap in the rocks.

Mary Wicker married the Revd Sir Thomas Delves Broughton in 1766 and they set up home together at Broughton Hall, near Eccleshall in Staffordshire. Mary was intelligent and accomplished as well as beautiful and was depicted in a portrait by Sir Joshua Reynolds holding a sketchbook and pen. In May 1772 the couple set out on a grand tour together accompanied by her mother, Charlotte, a family friend, their five children and numerous servants. Mary kept a detailed diary of their travels through France, Belgium, the Netherlands and Switzerland. It is a fascinating record of the galleries and museums they visited along with details of everyday social history, including observations of children dressed like Egyptian mummies and that in Switzerland 'one of the maids was catch'd pidling in the stew pan'.

The Broughtons' eldest son, Sir John Delves Broughton, married Elizabeth Egerton (1771–1857). When they separated in 1814, Elizabeth, then known as Dame Eliza Broughton, moved to Hoole House in Chester, where she poured her energies into creating a most astonishing garden. The lawn and bedding displays were spectacular but of more interest to John and Jane Loudon on their 1838 visit was the rock garden. This was described by Jane in an 1842 issue of *Ladies' Magazine of Gardening* as:

Perhaps the most remarkable and best executed rock garden in existence. It is formed on a level surface, and consists of an imitation or miniature copy of the

Swiss glaciers; with a valley between, into which the mountain scenery projects and retires, forming several beautiful and picturesque openings, which are diversified by scattered fragments of rock of various shapes and sizes, and by mountain trees and shrubs, and other plants.

The walls and foundations of the rock garden were mostly built of the local red sandstone. John Loudon described some of the difficulties that the gardeners had had to overcome which included, 'rain washed away the soil, and frost swelled the stones: several times the main wall failed from the weight put upon it'. Part of the garden was designed to represent the Mer de Glace in Chamonix with grey limestone and quartz. This had no planting and gaps between rocks were filled with broken fragments of white marble to give the impression of snow. On the lower slopes were planted a 'selection of the most beautiful and rare alpines'. The cultivation needs of each species were carefully considered with pockets of soil modified with moss or clean-washed river gravel according to moisture requirements.

Dame Eliza spent nearly forty years perfecting her garden to her own personal satisfaction. Her motivation for wanting a replica glacier on her doorstep is unclear but she was reluctant to have it publicised as it was close to the house and she dreaded day-trippers coming to see it. After she died the American horticulturist Henry Winthrop Sargent made a special pilgrimage to Hoole House. In his book *Impressions of English Scenery* (1865) he described meeting an old gardener who showed him the garden which was 'kept up just as Lady Broughton had left it ... when he had helped build and unbuild it as Lady Broughton was continually altering it'.

Loudon's writings about rock gardens inspired Sir Charles Edmund Isham (1819–1903) to create his own at Lamport Hall in Northamptonshire in 1847. Like that of Lady Broughton, his rock garden was built right against the hall so he could see it from his bedroom window. It was designed as a mountain in miniature with crevices, crystal caves made from quartz and dwarf trees. Isham did not dress his gardeners in alpine costumes but obviously believed his mountain needed inhabitants. He had travelled to Germany where in the 1840s there was something of a craze for ceramic gnomes; smaller versions of the dwarf sculptures of the Mirabell Gardens in Salzburg, Austria, created in 1715 for Prince Archbishop Franz Anton Harrach. Many of the Mirabell statues were modelled after people with dwarfism who lived in the court and served as entertainers to the archbishop. As representations of people with visible disabilities, the statues may be viewed today as cultural reminders of exploitation, but their popularity increased after they featured in the film *The Sound of Music*. Isham must have enjoyed the German gnomes as he brought a large number back to populate his rock garden. Some were purported to be hard at work mining the caves, whereas others had downed tools and were striking for fair pay. Family legend has it that Isham's daughters did not share his sense of humour or his love of gnomes and after his death the gnomes were shot to pieces with air rifles. Only one survived; known as Lampy, he now resides within the house.

The garden at Warley Place, near Brentwood in Essex, was one of the most celebrated of its time. It was the home of Ellen Ann Willmott (1858–1934), who moved there with her parents, Frederick and Ellen, and sister, Rose, in 1875. Ellen and Rose shared their mother's interest in gardening and now had a 30-acre estate in which to indulge their passion. Inspired by the mountain scenery she had seen in the Alps, Ellen started work on an alpine garden in 1882. The firm of James Backhouse was employed to build a ravine with rocks

Stone dwarf in the Mirabell Gardens, Vienna.

brought down from Yorkshire. A bridge was built to span the gorge and water flowed from a pond at the top into a southern pool, keeping the garden green and moist even in hot summers. She had a special cave created for her collection of filmy ferns. A path led down steps made from old milestones that Backhouse had bought from Cheshire County Council when they were installing new cast-iron mileposts in the 1890s.

Graham Stuart Thomas said of Willmott: 'She had beauty, intelligence, talent in many ways and the aptitude for complete absorption in whatever she was doing.' Her godmother, Countess Helen Tasker of Middleton Hall, died in 1888 leaving the sisters a substantial inheritance. Willmott was famed for her extravagance and spent huge amounts on plants for her gardens. At one time she employed over a hundred gardeners but was herself very much a hands-on gardener. She would often already be working away in the garden when the gardeners started to arrive and said, 'My plants and my gardens come before anything in my life for me and all my time is given up working in one garden and another, and when it is too dark to see the plants themselves I read or write about them.' She was friends with Henry Correvon of Geneva, who was four years older than her and acted as a mentor. He scolded her for including plants with double flowers in her garden and for spending too much money in his nursery, suggesting she could be sourcing plants locally or propagating them herself, but he tried to do what he could to help and permitted the head-hunting of one of his employees. In 1894 Willmott had observed the young gardener Jacob Maurer working diligently at Correvon's nursery and persuaded him to come to work for her with the promise of a cottage of his own and a pension of £1 per week once he retired. Maurer took her up on the offer, moving into the South Lodge to which he brought his Swiss wife and where they raised their family of nine children. Willmott had an alpine propagating

37

house built in response to Correvon's suggestion and a crocus lawn planted like the alpine meadows suggested by William Robinson.

Willmott was highly regarded by her contemporaries. The botanist William Stearn wrote that at Warley Place she 'grew some one hundred thousand different kinds of plants supremely well'. She was described by Gertrude Jekyll as 'the greatest of all living woman gardeners'. Both Jekyll and Willmott were awarded the Victoria Medal of Honour by the Royal Horticultural Society in 1897. Rose married into the Berkeley family and moved to Spetchley Park, near Worcester, where many of her sister's plants are still grown. Ellen Willmott is buried in the churchyard of the Catholic cathedral at Brentwood. After her death Warley Place was sold to pay for the debts that had accumulated from her prodigious spending. The house was demolished and the grounds are now maintained as a nature reserve.

Warley Place was not universally admired. Reginald Farrer said of Willmott's alpine gorge that it was 'to my own taste, a trifle too violent to be altogether pleasant'. One of the most determined of travellers, Reginald Farrer (1880–1920) has been called the 'Prince of Alpine Gardeners'. Growing up on the family estate of Ingleborough Hall in Clapham in Yorkshire, he was educated at home and developed an early interest in botany. At the age of fourteen he built his first rock garden in an old kitchen garden at his family home. While studying at Oxford he helped the Revd Henry Jardine Bidder with the rock garden at St John's College. After graduating in 1902, he travelled to Japan and Korea, writing *The Garden of Asia* (1904) about his experiences. Then came a series of trips to Switzerland, France, Italy and Austria, searching for alpine plants that would grow in the British climate. He used these to stock the Craven Nursery Company that he established with help from his mother.

Raised alpine bed at Spetchley Park in Worcestershire.

It was Farrer's 1907 book *My Rock Garden* that brought him to the attention of the gardening public and did much to fuel the British rock garden trend. He had a very forthright way of speaking which showed in his writings. He gave disparaging descriptions of the rockeries in vogue at the time, distinguishing between those of the 'dog's grave' and 'almond pudding' types. Plants that he admired were described in glowing terms but those he disliked were referred to as miffs, mimps or squinny. The hauntingly beautiful but tricky to grow oncocyclus iris were described as 'silken sad uncertain queens' and 'chief mourners in their own funeral-pomps'. He could be less than complimentary about other gardeners too. Even those he liked tended to receive rather back-handed compliments. Of Wolley Dod's garden he wrote, 'that marvellous garden of his made little claim to artistic construction (much of it being like three magnified and stony potato ridges), yet the beauty of the stone employed completed the attraction of those splendid plants of his.'

In 1908 Farrer and his friend Aubrey Herbert travelled to Sri Lanka, where Farrer became a Buddhist. Before the First World War, he teamed up with Kew-trained plantsman William Purdom, spending two years collecting plants and seeds in China on the border with Tibet. Farrer always travelled with the complete works of Jane Austen, whisky and an ample supply of peppermint creams. His magnum opus was *The English Rock Garden*, first published in 1919. That year he left for a plant-hunting expedition in Upper Burma. In a letter to his cousin, Osbert Sitwell, he wrote, 'So now I'm happy as the day is long, working hard among the plants and camping on high passes, full of snow and midges.' Conditions were bitterly cold with incessant rain and Farrer fell ill, dying on 17 October 1920. He was buried by the Gurkha Bhanje Bhaju at Kawngglanghpu. His mother had a memorial erected on which was written: 'He died for love and duty, in search of rare plants.' Today Farrer is remembered in the names of many alpine plants such as the exquisite blue *Gentiana farreri*, and with the Farrer Medal, which is awarded to the best plant at the Alpine Garden Society's shows.

One of Farrer's sponsors for his plant-hunting expedition to Yunnan and Kansu in China in 1914 was Sir Frederick Stern. Born into a wealthy banking family, Stern had attended university at Christ Church, Oxford. As a young man he enjoyed big game hunting in Africa and the Americas. In 1909 he leased Highdown Tower, near Worthing, and began to create a garden out of the surrounding chalk pits. He approached the botanist Clarence Elliot, a friend of Farrer, to assist with building a rockery. Having been told that nothing of beauty would grow on chalk, Stern was determined to prove the doubters wrong and Highdown became a growing obsession. He funded several plant hunters including George Forrest, Dora Stafford and Frank Kingdon-Ward, creating a fascinating garden that attracted streams of visitors. Stern was highly regarded for his monographs on *Paeonia* and *Galanthus* and *Leucojum* and his book for gardeners *A Chalk Garden*, published in 1960.

The plant explorer Frank Kingdon-Ward (1885–1958) had himself built a large rockery at his home Hatton Gore, now under the east end of London's Heathrow Airport. It was designed to look like a bend in a river ravine in the Himalayas and must have brought back memories of his adventures on plant-hunting trips. He described in the *Scottish Geographical Magazine* (1913) how 'one day in a mist I was pursued by a bull yak, and on another occasion in the forest I found myself face to face with a black bear. Then we had a wedding, and the whole village got gloriously drunk; also a funeral, and they got

The soft blue flowers of the Himalayan poppy (*Meconopsis*).

drunker'. Kingdon-Ward is associated with the ethereal beauty of the blue Himalayan poppy, described in his 1913 book *The Land of the Blue Poppy*.

Unlike some of her male plant-collecting colleagues, Dora Stafford was an expert high-altitude mountain climber. She spent long periods based at Arequipa in Peru during the 1930s collecting for the British Museum and Kew, Edinburgh and Copenhagen botanical gardens. She commented that, 'One advantage of the great height was that food keeps fresh and good for an extraordinary long time. An egg, for instance, is still perfectly good a month after being laid.' The plant of *Bidens triplinervia* that Frederick Stern planted in his rock garden was collected by Stafford from the mountains of Peru. In 1937 she collected the daisy relative *Xenophyllum staffordiae* in San Antonio de Esquilache, near Puno, and this was named after her by Peruvian botanists.

4

No Stone Unturned

The rock garden at Chelsea Physic Garden is generally acknowledged to have been one of the first constructed specifically for growing alpine plants but was used just for teaching apprentices of the Worshipful Society of Apothecaries. The garden did not fully open to the public until 1987. From the Victorian era though there were gardens that could be enjoyed by anyone and rock gardens became an increasingly popular feature of botanic and demonstration gardens. From public parks and the landscaped surroundings of holiday camps, everyone could get inspiration for their own rock garden.

Snowdrops at the Chelsea Physic Garden.

THE ROCKERY, VICTORIA PARK

Victoria Park in Tower Hamlets (opened 1845) is London's oldest public park. The rockery, pictured in 1912, provided interest for strollers.

Kew Gardens were first opened to the public in 1840 when they were transferred from the Crown to the care of the government. A rock garden had been built there with Reigate sandstone in 1867 but the present rock garden dates to around 1882. It was built to accommodate more than 2,500 alpine plants bequeathed by George Curling Joad (1837–81), a rope maker and shipping agent whose leisure activities included playing croquet and plant collecting. The garden was designed to simulate a meandering rocky watercourse in the Pyrenees with a charmingly named 'dripping well' as a feature. Rocks of Cheddar limestone were laid to mimic natural geological stratification. When the curator Walter Irving published *Rock Gardening* in 1925 he reported that when the rock garden was remodelled, further limestone was brought in from Derbyshire, Yorkshire and Westmorland. The air pollution then prevalent in London restricted the growth of lichens and mosses, so the limestone mostly remained glaringly white. George Preston, curator of the Alpine and Herbaceous Department in the 1950s, had the rock garden rebuilt using the more subdued Sussex sandstone. The rock gardens at Kew continue to evolve with new waterfalls created in 1994 and the dramatic Davies Alpine House landscape opened in 2006.

The Royal Botanic Garden Edinburgh was founded in 1670 as a physic garden to grow medicinal plants in Holyrood. It moved in 1820 to the 70-acre site at Inverleith Row. Many of the mature trees made the journey using a transplanting machine drawn by twelve horses. The first rock garden was built by James McNab using stone from a wall which had previously separated the botanical garden from an old experimental garden,

42

The rockery at Kew Gardens with attendant.

The Rock Garden, Kew Gardens.

Young visitors to the Rock Garden at Kew.

with additional stone taken from dismantled buildings in Edinburgh, as well as basalt columns from the Isle of Staffa and the Giant's Causeway. It was designed as a series of separate compartments, each planted with a single alpine specimen. Described as 'looking well' by Adam White in the *Edinburgh Evening Courant* of 18 April 1870, he particularly praised the variety of colours of scilla, including *Scilla siberica* – 'like a coy maiden'. The garden was studded with a number of small mounds, each topped with a monkey puzzle tree (*Araucaria araucana*), which were extremely popular at the time. McNab named each mound after a famous alpine botanist. The rock garden was redeveloped in 1914 to create a more natural-looking display with a waterfall feeding a stream that runs through the garden. A moraine, or scree bed, was added at the front in 1933 to accommodate alpines from the Sino-Himalaya region.

William King, Archbishop of Dublin from 1703 to 1729, declared that 'when any couple had a mind to be wicked, they would retire to Glasnevin'. Ireland's first botanic gardens at Glasnevin were designed though not for wickedness but to advance knowledge of plants for agricultural, medicinal and dyeing purposes. Researchers working at the gardens were the first to identify the infection responsible for the 1845–47 Irish Potato Famine. A plan of the garden from 1800 shows a mount in the centre of the herbaceous borders which was studded with rocks accommodating 'saxatile and rock plants'. At the end of the 1880s a rock garden was constructed using stone quarried at the nearby Finglas Quarry. Reginald Farrer, perhaps thinking of that early Glasnevin devilry, described it, and the one at Edinburgh, as the finest examples of what he called the 'Devil's Lapful' style of rock garden: 'The plan is simplicity itself. Take a hundred or a thousand cartloads of bare square-faced boulders. You next drop them about absolutely anyhow: and you then plant things amongst them. The chaotic hideousness of the result is something to be remembered with shudders ever after.'

View of the rock garden at the Royal Botanic Gardens Edinburgh, *c.* 1911.

Geographical planting in the rock garden at Edinburgh, 2023.

Raised bed and alpine houses at Edinburgh, 2023.

James Backhouse of York was employed at Birmingham Botanical Gardens to build their rock garden in 1893. He used 250 tonnes of millstone grit, transported in part by narrowboats on the Worcester and Birmingham Canal. The £650 cost was financed by local factory owners the Nettlefold family, who had their own rock garden built at Winterborne. In 2019 a new alpine garden was designed with a network of pathways dividing the area into themed sections. The central limestone outcrop is planted with Turkish meadow plants.

The rock garden at Wisley, the Surrey home of the Royal Horticultural Society, was constructed between 1910 and 1912 by James Pulham and Son, working to designs by the landscape architect Edward White. It used 550 tonnes of Sussex sandstone including boulders up to 2 tonnes in weight. These required the building of temporary railway tracks to get them across the garden from the Portsmouth Road. The garden includes a stream, a series of small waterfalls and a grotto for ferns. It was planted with dwarf conifers and small weeping trees to provide year-round interest, including the cloud-pruned Japanese larch, thought to be the oldest-surviving plant at Wisley. A wide range of alpine perennials

Edelweiss growing at the Alan King alpine garden at Birmingham Botanic Garden.

The rock garden at Wisley, Surrey, in May 2010.

Autumn crocus flowering in the alpine meadow at Wisley.

such as species of peonies, iris and primula are grown, interspersed with small bulbs and cyclamen. The alpine meadow at the bottom of the rock garden was planted in the late 1920s with thousands of bulbs such as *Narcissus bulbocodium* and autumn crocus.

At Cambridge Botanic Gardens the earliest rock garden was made with a mixture of stones including old masonry stone and a sham gothic arch. This and the main rock garden, built before the First World War of Oxfordshire sandstone, were removed when the limestone rock garden was constructed in the late 1950s. Under the direction of John Gilmour, rocks for the new garden, some weighing up to 3 tonnes, were brought from the Lake District. The planting was laid out geographically to represent the mountain floras of Europe, Asia, America, South Africa and Australasia and includes such treasures as the Himalayan peony (*Paeonia emodi*) as well as familiar European species including edelweiss and the native pasque flower (*Pulsatilla vulgaris*). Graham Stuart Thomas writing in 1989 was not impressed, saying, 'it is a pity that this outlandish rock garden was allowed to intrude on the peaceful classic design of over a hundred years' standing.'

Oxford Botanic Garden, founded in 1621, is the oldest botanic garden in the United Kingdom, created with four thousand cartloads of 'mucke and dunge' to raise the soil level above the Cherwell floodplain for the first beds of medicinal plants. The rock garden

Alpine plants in front of the glasshouses at Cambridge Botanical Gardens.

was constructed in 1926 with 125 tonnes of sandstone brought from Tubney, 6 miles west of Oxford. The garden has been recently redesigned to display plants in homage to Oxford-born John Sibthorp (1758–96), whose travels in the eastern Mediterranean led to the publication of the lavishly illustrated *Flora Graeca*.

The seventeenth-century Newby Hall first opened to paying visitors in 1948, but by that time the previously glorious rock garden had suffered periods of neglect. Robert Charles de Grey Vyner (1842–1915) was keenly interested in rock gardens and his library included Robinson's *Alpine Flowers*, David Wooster's *Alpine Plants* and Farrer's *The English Rock Garden*. Vyner and his wife Nelly were friends of Ellen Willmott and exchanged presents of plants and game. In the late 1890s they had the rock garden built by Backhouse of York to a design by Willmott. Massive boulders of millstone grit from the Yorkshire Dales were used with interest created from carved medieval stones including pinnacles from York Minster obtained during the rolling programme of restoration work at the cathedral. A stone aqueduct was built to carry water from a water tower above the house to a series of pools and streams.

Vyner's grandson, Major Edward Compton, restored the garden in the 1930s, reporting that, 'Nearly every plant of value in the Rock Garden had succumbed to the 1914/1918 war neglect'. The rock garden has undergone another restoration since 2021. Overgrown conifers were cleared to let in sunlight and open up vistas. Original plant labels found during the restoration show that previous plantings included such popular rock garden perennials as *Campanula pusilla* and *Salix serpyllifolia*.

49

Thomas William Simpson was a businessman who had made his fortune in the margarine industry. He bought Compton Acres House near Poole in Dorset in 1920, along with 10 acres of heathland. A keen traveller, Simpson set out to create a series of themed gardens to reflect places he had visited, including an Italian garden and a homage to the American desert, planted with cacti and succulents. The rock garden areas used contrasting red sandstone and grey limestone, separated by stone-flagged paths. The highlight was the Japanese garden inspired by a visit to the gardens at Kyoto. He imported genuine stone and bronze artefacts such as snow lanterns. Japanese landscape gardeners were employed to supervise the work. A thatched tea house was erected at the top of stone steps and plantings included Japanese wisteria (*Wisteria floribunda*), Kurume hybrid azaleas, Japanese cherries and acer. Even the koi for the pond were specially imported. The gardens were opened to the public soon after completion up until the outbreak of the Second World War. Simpson died in 1944 and the gardens have since been in the care of a number of different owners but continue to attract many thousands of visitors.

After its Regency heyday, the number of visitors to the city of Bath had fallen and a public park was proposed to attract more visitors and encourage people to move there to live. The Bath Corporation gave £100 per annum towards upkeep of the park, with the rest of the funds raised by voluntary contributions. The new park was opened in 1830 by the young Princess Victoria and named the Royal Victoria Park. The 9 acres included a number of trees and shrubs, herbaceous borders and a scented walk. A rocky dell was created out of an old quarry and was planted with conifers. The present botanic garden was laid out in 1887 to home a collection of 2,000 herbaceous and alpine plants that had been presented to the Victoria Park Committee on the death of Christopher Edmund Broome (1812–86). His botanical specimens and library were bequeathed to the Bath Royal Literary and Scientific Institution. The garden was laid out by John Milburn who came from Kew to do the work and later became park superintendent. He had a shallow ravine dug on a slope and lined it with large limestone rocks similar to those at Kew.

The public park movement in the United Kingdom arose in the 1830s from a desire to improve the health of workers living in the overcrowded conditions of the industrial cities. The first park in England to be built wholly with taxpayer money was Birkenhead Park in Merseyside. It was designed by Joseph Paxton who based the rockery on the one he had created for Chatsworth House, aiming to give the impression of a rock fall in the Alps, with a view to the Swiss-styled bridge beyond. The park was opened by Lord Morpeth on Easter Monday 1847 with thousands of people attending the ceremony. Three years later Frederick Law Olmsted, a landscape architect from the United States, visited the park, admiring the 'masses of rock-work, and mosses and rock-plants attached to them'. He commented, 'And all this magnificent pleasure ground is entirely, unreservedly, and for ever, the people's own. The poorest British peasant is as free to enjoy it in all its parts as the British queen.' Olmsted used Birkenhead as a model for his design for Central Park in New York.

The Promenade Gardens at St Annes-on-the-Sea in Lancashire has a rockery that runs along the beachward side of the gardens. The gardens were laid out by the Pulham firm in 1913–14. They created an informal lake with stepping stones and bridges, a grotto and an impressive waterfall, using nearly 1,000 tonnes of rock from Derbyshire and Clitheroe. Salt-tolerant shrubs such as tamarisks and hedging were planted to provide some protection from the harsh sea winds for the herbaceous and rockery plants.

Above: Botanical garden at the Royal Victoria Park, Bath, 1905.

Below: A gentleman in a bowler hat strolls through the rock garden at the Royal Victoria Park, Bath, 1905.

Families enjoying the rockery at Birkenhead Park.

View of the bridge and rock garden at St Annes-on-the-Sea.

Children enjoying the rock garden at St Annes-on-the-Sea.

The Belper River Gardens in Derbyshire also feature the work of the Pulhams. The gardens date from 1905 when the Belper Boating Association was formed with support from cotton-mill-owner George Herbert Strutt. He donated land that had been used to grow willow osiers used in his North Mill. The ground was landscaped with a riverside promenade, teahouse and a bandstand. The Pulhams made a fountain and rockwork pool along the winding 'Serpentine Walk'. In 1918, after the demise of the Boating Association, Strutt gave the gardens to the English Sewing Cotton Company to use as leisure facilities for its workers and public recreation.

One of the most widely applauded of the early municipal rock gardens was Happy Valley at Great Orme's Head in Llandudno in north Wales. The site was originally a quarry, but in 1887 it was donated to the town of Llandudno by Lord Mostyn to mark Queen Victoria's golden jubilee. The rock garden was built in the late 1920s by the park superintendent, W. G. Robertson, with a series of rockwork terraces. Over a thousand species and cultivars were grown, all carefully labelled. The Llandudno Town Improvement Society produced a catalogue of many of the plants growing there, with notes on rock garden construction and planting advice for home gardeners. The plants included edelweiss, lewisias and South African ixias, which, as the booklet explained, needed a sheltered position. The Gorsedd Stones (Cerrig yr Orsedd), a group of standing stones, were constructed for the 1963 National Eisteddfod of Wales.

Emily Williamson (1855–1936), who with Eliza Phillips founded the Royal Society for the Protection of Birds in 1891, lived for thirty years at Croft in Didsbury, Manchester. Both Emily and her husband, Robert, were keen botanists and often travelled to the Alps in Europe

The rockwork at the Belper River Gardens was the work of the Pulham firm, seen here around 1906.

The rock gardens at Skegness were very popular with tourists to the town in the early twentieth century.

where they collected many plants. They created a rockery on the sheltered south-facing slope of their garden and used this as a place to grow their finds. The Williamsons moved to Brook in Surrey in 1912 taking many of their alpine plants with them but rock gardening remains an important part of what is now Fletcher Moss Park, named after local alderman Fletcher Moss, who donated the property to the city of Manchester in 1915.

Chesterfield in Derbyshire is best known for the wonderful twisted spire of its church but for a while it too had a rock garden which was described in the *Derbyshire Courier* of Saturday 15 May 1909: 'the pretty little Alpine garden in front of the fine old Church and abutting one of the busiest street of the town, is one of the biggest small improvements which have been carried out in Chesterfield for many years.' It had been built at the instigation of Thomas Philpot Wood, a wine merchant and town councillor, who donated £500 of his own money towards the garden. Upkeep proved to be difficult and not everyone was enthusiastic. By 1912 Councillor Lancaster declared that it was the most ugly spot in Chesterfield and wanted the stones moved to make 'a nice flower bed'. The garden was moved in 1915 to expand a roadway to the church and demolished in 1931.

The alpine gardens in front of Chesterfield's famous church spire.

Chesterfield Church and Alpine Gardens

55

The extensive rock gardens at Pwllheli holiday camp.

The first of the Butlin's holiday camps was opened by Billy Butlin in 1936 in Skegness. The camp near Pwllheli in Wales opened in the 1940s and could accommodate 12,000 campers at its peak in the late 1960s. Rock gardens were created as part of the initial landscaping and used local stone. They sloped away from the chalets, with paths leading down to the pond. The planting was dominated by easy to grow mat-forming species such as snow-in-summer (*Cerastium tomentosum*). The gardens were often decorated, not just plants, but also the contenders for the title of holiday princess. The camp is now a Haven caravan park, but the gardens remain.

In the United States, Smith College in Northampton, Massachusetts, was founded in 1871 with an endowment from Sophia Smith. Smith wanted young women to receive the same academic and intellectual training as men. The first president, Laurenus Clark Seelye, believed in the importance of a scientific education for women. He transformed the college campus into an arboretum and botanic garden, employing the landscape architecture firm F. L. Olmsted & Company in 1892. The garden's first director, William Francis Ganong, took over the task of planting the arboretum, establishing the systematic beds and building a rock garden. A newer innovation is the Rock Park, suggested by geology professor John Brady. Working with landscape architect Nancy W. Denig, he designed a curated rock collection which tells the story of the geological history of the north-eastern United States.

An editorial in the *Wilmington News-Journal* in Ohio suggested in June 1931 a need to, 'establish a sort of Devils Island for people who make rock gardens and send all offenders there, giving them boulders and stink weed and daisies to work with until they are entirely cured'. This seems to have been largely ignored and in the 1930s the New York Botanical Garden built a rock garden with cascading waterfall and a stream. It has richly planted gravel beds, crevices for plants that like free drainage and woodland plants growing under mature trees. The Alpine Garden at the Montreal Botanic Garden, in Quebec, Canada, was a long time in the making. Work started in 1937, but it was not completed until 1962. The foundations were made of clinker, with sedimentary rocks used as the main stone. A newer development is a crevice garden built in spring 2005.

Rock gardens can be found around the world. The Hakgala Botanic Gardens at Hakgalla, Nuwara Eliya in Sri Lanka are situated at about 1750m above sea level and lie in the shadow of the Hakgala Rock (Elephant's jaw rock). The garden was established in 1861 by the English botanist and entomologist Dr George Henry Kendrick Thwaites (1811–82) for the experimental cultivation of Cinchona, several species of which yield quinine and other alkaloids. The gardens were subsequently used for tea production. The gardens have a cool temperate climate due to the high altitude. The gardens consist of several terraces allowing a huge range of species to be grown.

The rock garden at Hakgalla, Nuwara Eliya, Sri Lanka, with papyrus and waterlilies in the pond.

5

Mountains in Miniature

The domestic rock garden varies tremendously in style and size, reflecting the tastes and resources of the creator. Sir Frank Crisp (1843–1919) was certainly a man who had plenty of resources available. He was a lawyer and active member of the Royal Microscopical Society. In 1889 he bought two properties on the edge of Henley-on-Thames, Friar Park and Friar's Field, and employed the London architect Robert Clarke Edwards to rebuild Friar Park as a weekend retreat, commissioning landscape gardener Henry Ernest Milner to design the gardens. Crisp himself was very involved in the landscaping, with decided views on what he wanted. Told that he should not have made ponds on the side of a hill, he responded: 'it requires a degree of refinement in taste bordering on the fastidious to remove what is cheerful and pleasing to the eye, merely because it cannot be accounted for by the laws of Nature'.

Both the Pulham and Backhouse of York firms were involved in the creation of the rock garden. The design used 7,000 tonnes of Yorkshire millstone grit and included a 6-metre-high pastiche of the Matterhorn, surmounted by a piece taken from the actual mountain. At one time the garden contained around 4,000 alpine plants. The Pulhams made features including stepping stones, a rocking stone and a series of caves based on the ice caves at Grindelwald, some with artificial stalactites. The 'vine cave' was lit with lanterns in the shape of bunches of grapes and was lined with mirrors presenting optical illusions including 'withered and chained up hands' which supposedly represented those of 'a walled up Friar of a long past age'. Most famed was the 'gnome cave' populated by ceramic gnomes occupied in multifarious activities including taking snuff and one nursing his toothache. At the end of the cave another mirror reflected a distorted image of the visitor such that they were transformed into the figure of a gnome.

Crisp loved to share his enthusiasms. He opened the gardens to the public once a week in spring and summer and wrote an illustrated guide book. The 1910 edition had 276 pages and included information on plant taxonomy and anatomy. Alternatively, visitors could buy a fold-up guide published by Alan Tabor in around 1914. This annotated map showed the stables marked as 'ye abode of ye prancing steedes', centaurs frolicking in the paddock and a sign exhorting the visitor 'Don't keep off the grass'. Crisp was passionate about medieval history and his *Mediaeval Gardens* was published posthumously in 1924.

Contemporary views on Crisp's garden varied. Henry Correvon was an admirer and dedicated his book *Rock Garden and Alpine Plants* to Sir Frank and Lady Crisp. William Robinson said it was, 'the best natural stone rock garden I have ever seen'. However, Charles Thonger, in his *Book of Rock and Water Gardens* (1907), derided the 'absurd range of beetling crags and frowning cliffs', dismissing the garden as 'an Alpine peepshow, which might well serve as a sixpenny attraction at Earl's Court'. Reginald Farrer commented in the preface to E. A. Bowles' *My Garden in Spring*, 'This is a mosaic, this is a gambol in purple and gold; but it is not a rock garden, though tin chamois peer never so frequent from its cliffs upon the passer by.' Crisp was offended and responded in Robinson's magazine *Gardening Illustrated,* attacking Bowles in a horticultural war of words. After Crisp's death his garden went through periods of neglect before being purchased in 1970 by former Beatle George Harrison. Harrison's widow Olivia described how 'George used garden flame-throwers to clear the undergrowth and put two goats to clear the weeds and brambles on the rock garden'.

A more modest private rock garden was built for Frank Sayer Graham of Aysgarth in North Yorkshire in 1906. He was a game dealer and keen grower of tulips. He employed William Angus Clark (1858–1950), who had been the Backhouse alpine manager and worked on the rock garden at Friar Park. He created a walk-though grotto using limestone boulders probably taken from Stephen's Moor at Thornton Rust. Originally a small spring fed a cascade that ran down into a rill. The rock structure, up to 8 metres high, has narrow paths which pass under stone lintels and lead to an open space used initially as a vegetable garden. The garden was cared for by Frank and his wife, Mary, supported by gardener Herbert Robinson. When Mary died her sister, Annie, married Frank and took on the job of weeding the rock garden. It was very much a private garden with visitors by invitation only

The rockery in the village of Aysgarth as featured in a vintage postcard.

Above: The Edwardian rock garden in 2023.

Below: Aysgarth rock garden.

Above: A secluded bench surrounded by rocks and plants.

Below: The Aysgarth rock garden remains open to the public.

and children strictly forbidden. Sometimes tourists would be shown round in exchange for a donation to charity.

As is so often the case, when the original owners died the garden became neglected. However, as an important example of an Edwardian rock garden, it became Grade II listed in 1988 to protect the rockwork and the iron railings that surround the garden. In recent years it has been restored to its former glory with a selection of lime-tolerant plants used to give a long season of interest, including ferns, primulas and spring- and autumn-flowering bulbs. It is open to the public for a voluntary donation throughout the year and remains a charming place to spend a summer evening, peacefully cocooned by rock.

Many alpine enthusiasts start with a small bed of alpine plants, only to find that as their interest deepens the rock garden expands. John McCrindle, a native of the village of Dunure in South Ayrshire with a strong interest in natural history, was one such. His rock garden spread to encompass the whole of the roadside front garden. It became a tourist attraction and surviving picture postcards show that for a while a tea garden was provided for thirsty visitors. *The Journal of the Glasgow and Andersonian Natural History and Microscopical Scociety* reported that on 2 April 1945 McCrindle led an excursion for members which started with a tour of his garden where many interesting plants including the Canadian bloodroot (*Sanguinaria canadensis*) were in flower. In 1946 he was reported to have attended a meeting in Glasgow to revive the Scottish Rock Garden Club after the war 'strikingly dressed in his fisherman's dark blue jersey'. In 2008 McCrindle's treasured garden was dismantled and the stones donated to outline the Dunure Labyrinth built near the castle ruins.

John McCrindle's rock garden at Dunure, as illustrated in a tinted vintage postcard.

Plants in Pots, Sinks and Troughs

In 1597 Jan Govertsz van der Aar, a Dutch collector of plants and shells declared, in a letter to the botanist Carolus Clusius: 'I desire things that are rare and appealing and I covet colourful flowers; the rarer they are, the more covetous I am.' That desire for rarity has not abated in the intervening centuries. However, unlike the collector of shells, those who accumulate rare plants have to try to keep them alive. John Loudon grew over 600 species of alpines in his London garden and, like many early growers of alpines, kept all of them in pots. Growing plants in pots made it easier to individualise the growing conditions. In 1853 Charles McIntosh suggested in *The Book of the Garden* that standard compost should equal parts of sandy peat and loam but for some alpines such as *Saxifraga cernua* it would be better to use 'soil in which mica in a reduced state forms a part'.

Simple ceramic pots for plants were being produced by the early eighteenth century. John Morton, in *The Natural History of Northamptonshire* (1712), described the local clays including an inferior blue clay used for tiles 'and ordinary garden pots'. He reported that 'the garden pots made of it tho' never so well baked, are apt to scale, and be broken in pieces by foul weather and frosts: but being sized, that is, laid in oil, will bide the weather as well as any whatsoever as the sellers of them say, but others who made that experiment have found it fail them'. Writers disagreed on whether glazed or unglazed pots were best. George William Johnson's *A Dictionary of Modern Gardening* (1846) declared that 'the prejudice against glazed pots is now exploded ... Stoneware and china-ware are infinitely preferable, for they keep the roots more uniformly moist and warm'. However, Robert Thompson, in *The Gardener's Assistant* of 1878, was concerned that roots receive less aeration in a glazed pot.

The shape of the pot is also significant. Some plants such as houseleeks will grow well in shallow alpine pans but deep pots, known as long toms, are preferred for plants with extensive, searching roots. These probably originated in the Netherlands for growing hyacinths and other bulbs. Special double pots were also made for alpine plants. These had an inner vessel

An expertly grown example of the Primula hybrid 'Lismore Jewel', potted for display on the show bench.

63

inside a larger one. The inner pot had a drainage hole whereas the outer was not pierced so that water or damp moss could be placed in it to keep the plant cool. From the 1960s onwards the use of light plastic pots became more common, although with modern concerns about sustainability, alternative materials such as bamboo are increasingly sought today.

Sinks and troughs have been used to grow alpine plants since Victorian times and enable the creation of miniature alpine landscapes. Clarence Elliott visited Mrs Saunders of Wennington Hall in Lancashire in the 1890s and admired her use of an old stone trough as a planter, filled with river sand and leaf mould as the growing medium. He started exhibiting trough gardens at Chelsea in 1923, and they quickly became popular. When

Left: Plants such as this *Sempervivum ciliosum* var. *galicicum* can be grown successfully in a shallow alpine pan.

Below: Alpines planted in an antique stone trough at Spetchley Park, near Worcester.

the supply of stone sinks inevitably reduced, the use of hypertufa, a mixture of peat moss, Portland cement and sand, enabled porcelain sinks to be coated to look like old stone ones. Even polystyrene fish boxes suitably treated with hypertufa are used and have the advantage that they are much lighter to move.

Right: Display of planted troughs by D'Arcy & Everest at the London Show, 2010.

Below: Troughs by the alpine house at Royal Botanic Garden Edinburgh.

Alpine Houses and Bulb Frames

Serious growers of high alpine plants have to consider many aspects of the plants' requirements. In places where winters can be mild and wet, there is a need to reproduce the snow cover that such plants would receive in their native habitat. Early growers plunged potted plants outdoors in ash-pits, protecting them from rain with glass bell-jars or cold-frames covered with glass sashes. Farrer was not a fan and declined to grow plants that required protection such as calochortus, oncocyclus iris and lewisia, saying, 'The moment glass frames and bells and fussments begin to cover your ground gone is all the air of simple happiness that makes a garden joyful; and, instead, you have a constrained look, as of a kindergarten or a reformatory.'

George Maw (1832–1912) of Benthall Hall in Shropshire ran Maw & Co. ceramic tile company. In 1868 he patented a particularly durable plant label 'made of burnt earthenware, either composed of pulverised clay by Prosser's process or of plastic clay'. Maw's interests included botany, geology and archaeology. He travelled widely in Turkey, North Africa and America and accompanied Sir Joseph Dalton Hooker on a plant-hunting expedition to the Moroccan Atlas Mountains in 1871. Maw had a particular interest in crocus and while working on his 1886 monograph on the genus grew most of the then known species in an enormous cold frame. This was the forerunner of modern bulb frames. Frames can be at ground level or, to save the gardener's back, built as raised beds with glazing to protect from the rain but plenty of ventilation to prevent overheating.

Glasshouses had become much cheaper after the repeal of the glass tax in 1845 and huge interest was generated by the Great Exhibition in London. Specialist alpine houses were designed particularly to protect alpine plants from wet conditions in winter and of course have the added advantage of providing shelter for the gardener and any visitors. They require excellent ventilation but are often unheated as the plants grown are usually hardy, requiring protection only from hard frosts. Shading may be needed in sunny conditions.

The first alpine house at Kew opened in 1887. It was a wooden construction with a low ridge. Plants were displayed in pots on benches with shading provided by roll-down blinds on the outside of the structure. In 1981 a pyramidal alpine house was built to display landscaped plantings of small shrubs and bulbs in tufa rock. It had a refrigerated bench to provide a cool root run for arctic alpines. The Davies Alpine House was opened in 2006. It was designed by Wilkinson Eyre Architects using technology inspired by the natural cooling strategy seen in termite ant nests in order to dispense with the need for energy-intensive air-conditioning units.

The Wisley alpine houses include a specialist cushion house for the display of more than 300 cushion alpines such as *Androsace* and *Dionysia*, which are planted directly into tufa rock. At the Cambridge Botanic Gardens the Mountains House is home to a variety of high-altitude alpines and bulbous plants including National Collections of *Fritillaria, Tulipa* and *Saxifraga*. The alpine house at Harlow Carr in Yorkshire was one of the first large-scale projects to be accomplished, when the Royal Horticultural Society took on the care of the garden in 2001. Rock from a previous sandstone rock garden was re-used to construct the display beds. Plants grown include gentians, vibrant scarlet *Jamesbrittenia bergae* and bulbs such as South African nerines. A new alpine house at the Birmingham Botanic Garden contains tufa rock cliffs, which are planted with many species to complement the National Collection of Cyclamen which is displayed in the older house.

Above: Cold frames at Royal Botanic Garden Edinburgh.

Below: The alpine houses at Royal Botanic Garden Edinburgh.

Above: Plants in the alpine house at Leicester Botanic Garden.

Below: Alpine house at Birmingham Botanic Garden.

Moraines, Screes and Crevices

The grounds of Farrer's Ingleborough Hall have a crescent-shaped bank of natural glacial moraine deposits. This may have inspired Farrer to build his artificially-made scree gardens that he referred to as 'moraine'. His 'Old Moraine' in the lower part of the Craven Nursery rock garden was so successful that he created another moraine within his private rock garden. In geological parlance moraine is the loose sediment and rock debris deposited by glacier ice, whereas scree is a collection of broken rock fragments at the base of a cliff, but gardeners tend to use the words interchangeably, with scree used more commonly nowadays. Farrer was not the first to create such a feature; in Austria a monk named Gottwald had made something similar in 1835. In the 1890s Farrer helped Edward Augustus Bowles to plan a moraine in the rock garden at Myddelton House in Middlesex and together they assisted the plant collector Frederick J. Hanbury (1851–1935) with his rock garden at Brockhurst in West Sussex.

Hanbury described his moraine in *A Sussex Rock-garden* in 1919. He had made a series of cement tanks containing valves that were closed in summer but left to drain in winter allowing the moisture level to be controlled. Filled with moraine material, these tanks allowed Hanbury to grow plants such as *Gentiana verna* and *G. acaulis* and the native Teesdale violet, *Viola arenaria*. He reported that, 'The plant attains finer proportions in my moraine than it does where I found it in Teesdale'.

Dorothy Graham (1898–1966) created Branklyn Garden on the side of Kinnoull Hill in Perth with her husband, John. Dorothy was interested in the plants being sent from the Himalaya by collectors such as George Forrest and Frank Kingdon Ward. She had their tennis court dug up to make way for a rockery with boulders quarried from Kinnoull Hill and gravel from the River Tay. She found the free-draining nature of her scree beds particularly beneficial for growing alpines: 'If a good plant of any kind appears dissatisfied and unhappy where it has been planted, it generally becomes a rejuvenated specimen when transferred to the scree.'

Moraine or scree gardens try to replicate the free-draining conditions found on the mountainside as on Mount Parnassus in Greece where *Ranunculus brevifolius* grows.

The crevice garden at Wisley, 2013.

Crevice gardens have become a popular trend in rock gardening, inspired particularly by gardeners in the Czech Republic. Czech specialist Zdenék Zvolanék worked with Joyce Carruthers from Canada at the Denver Botanic Gardens' alpine garden on Mount Goliath. This inspired many others around the world. Crevice gardens typically have raised level areas set with flat rocks to create a pavement-like surface with crevices between the stones for alpine plants. One of the largest crevice gardens is that at Bangsbo Botanic Garden in Frederikshavn in the north of Denmark. It used 200 tonnes of limestone imported from a quarry in southern Germany and 3,500 plants arranged geographically. At the Nezahat Gökyiğit Botanical Garden in Istanbul the plantings in the crevice garden concentrate on Turkish endemics. Located at the top of a hill, this allows the study of native plants while enjoying the views of the surrounding city.

Sempervivums growing in the crevices between pieces of slate at Utrecht Botanic Garden in the Netherlands.

Matters of Taste

'All rock gardeners are snobs,' wrote Elizabeth Lawrence of Charlotte, North Carolina, while considering the peculiar passion for the miniature and perfect, adding, 'I say this without fear of offending, for no one will take it to himself. "How right you are," he will say. "I have often noticed it in one or another, and there are times when I think you are something of a snob yourself."' Lawrence, a garden writer and the first woman graduate in landscape architecture at the North Carolina State University, thought that some snobbery should be expected as the cultivation of alpine plants was 'the highest form of the art of gardening.'

In 1856 Shirley Hibberd pilloried gardeners who tried to imitate the rockeries they saw in London parks in their own gardens. He criticised particularly those made of bricks and flints and daubed in paint, saying, 'The mere mention of rock-work is usually sufficient to raise a smile on the face of an enthusiast in gardening; for of all the mistakes that are made by amateurs and even by professed gardeners and landscapists, the Rockery is but too frequently the most ridiculous.' The alpine specialist Will Ingwersen also had strong views on rocks, suggesting in the *Gardening Illustrated* of June 1952, 'The simplest basic rule for use in building a rock garden that I know of is to remember always that the rocks, whether large or small, whether outcropping or in bold and continuous arrangement, should look as if they have been there since the beginning of time.' Of course, not everyone could have a rock garden built by Backhouse of York, whose nursery rock garden created in 1859 was seen as the most excellent exemplar.

Frederick Edward Hulme, Professor of Drawing at King's College London and a keen botanist, acknowledged that, 'something of the nature of a rockery, or rather brickery, may be sometimes seen compounded of old brickbats, lumps of cement, clinkers, and masses

The gardeners at Utrecht Botanic Garden demonstrate what can be achieved with a 'well-planted clinkery' in reused drainage pipes.

of fused and vitrified material from the brickfield,' but added, 'while we cannot quite deny that a well-planted clinkery may be a good deal better than nothing at all, we feel at least equally strongly that it must be looked upon only as a possibility when nothing better can be got together.' Not everyone agreed of course, as Margery Fish knew to her cost, and even Alan Titchmarsh in 2015 wrote that rockeries were a way to use up unwanted rubble. Monty Don though, writing in July 2023, declared, 'I want the rockiness of a rockery, the great natural and architectural heft of slabs and chunks of stone. The rockeries I love are astonishingly ambitious affairs, and it is the scale of imagination and engineering that I admire as much as the horticultural outcome.'

These discussions about design of the rock garden, the balance between rock and plants, and even about the inclusion or prohibition of garden gnomes are really just matters of taste. One of the most respected garden writers of the United States, Louise Beebe Wilder, whose work *The Rock Garden* (1933) is considered a classic, did not tolerate snobbery saying, 'In the garden, every person may be their own artist without apology or explanation. Each within their green enclosure is a creator, and no two shall reach the same conclusion.'

Above left: A monumental 'scholar's rock' in the Huntington Botanical Garden in San Marino, California. (Image raisingourstars/Pixabay)

Above right: Wild *Erythronium dens-canis* in a natural rock garden in northern Greece.

The highly regarded Ness Botanic Gardens were founded by Arthur Kilpin Bulley.

73

The rockery at Ness Botanic Gardens. (Vintage Tucks postcard)

6

Rehabilitating the Rockery

The gardening section of the *Guardian* newspaper declared in April 2019 that a rockery revival was under way. Social media images fuelled a desire to build rock gardens which were promoted as being low maintenance and good for wildlife. The rock garden, like many other aspects of garden design, has certainly been subject to fashions. During the Victorian 'fern craze' ferns were the 'must-have' plant of the day and huge numbers were taken from the wild to grow in garden rockeries or fern houses. Rock garden plants too, and the ways in which they are used, have peaks and troughs in popularity. Indeed, a trough planted up with alpines may be on trend one year but considered somewhat passé the next. In your own garden, trends can be ignored but an awareness of the issues of conservation and sustainability are important for everyone.

In Victorian times country people could earn much-needed money selling wild plants to collectors, as in this painting, *The Fern Gatherer* by Charles Sillem Lidderdale (1877).

Plant Hunting and Conservation

When David Wooster, Assistant Secretary to the Museum of Natural History in Ipswich, published *Alpine Plants* in 1872 he warned that the English Lady's Slipper Orchid (*Cypripedium calceolus*) was 'in great danger of being altogether exterminated by the reprehensible avidity of collectors'. Wooster was right to be concerned. The orchid had never been widespread but previously occurred across the limestone districts of Derbyshire, Yorkshire, County Durham and Cumbria. Habitat changes, particularly woodland clearance, played a part, but the decline in the population of this species was primarily due to the collection of specimens by botanists and amateur enthusiasts. Just a solitary plant survived in North Yorkshire until English Nature's Species Recovery Programme got to work, increasing the population through management of habitats and artificial propagation techniques. The species has been planted at many additional locations to ensure its survival for future generations and it can now be admired growing at Kew Gardens.

Attitudes have changed since the time of the Victorian plant collectors and today most people agree with Wooster's comment, 'The practice of rooting up very rare plants cannot be too strongly deprecated.' Any botanist found plundering wild populations of rare plants would be ostracised by their peers. In England and Wales all wild plants are offered protection under the law and the Wildlife and Countryside Act of 1981 states this includes algae, fungi, lichens, mosses and liverworts as well as vascular plants. It is unlawful to uproot any wild plant without permission from the landowner and Sites of Special

Lady's Slipper Orchid.

Scientific Interest (SSSIs) are governed by further regulations. Owners and occupiers of such sites may be prosecuted if they destroy plants or remove plant material.

The Convention on International Trade in Endangered Species of Fauna and Flora (CITES) controls international trade in species that are at risk of extinction. It has two appendices: Appendix I lists species that cannot be traded for commercial purposes. Appendix II lists species that require a valid export permit before they can be traded commercially. Many common rock garden plants such as *Galanthus* and *Cyclamen* are listed in Appendix II. Since 12 October 2014 all plant material collected from the wild is covered by the United Nation's Nagoya Protocol. This ensures that utilisation of any wild-collected material, including the development of new named cultivars and hybrids, as well as production of novel drugs and other products, is only permitted with written consent from the country of origin. Simple plant cultivation, either privately or commercially, is not affected.

Climate change is a threat to wild populations of many rock garden plants, with the upward migration of plants occurring in alpine areas in response to increasing temperatures and lower levels of precipitation. Robert Amos, author of *International Conservation Law: The Protection of Plants in Theory and Practice,* emphasises that conservation has to be an ongoing process, 'We cannot afford to be complacent, even for those species that appear to be thriving'.

Rock garden societies can play a part in conservation. The constitution of Scottish Rock Garden Club for example, states that it exists 'to foster an interest in mountain and woodland plants and other plants and bulbs suitable for the rock garden, bog garden, wild garden or alpine house, to provide education about and increase and spread knowledge of such plants and to encourage their cultivation and preservation in gardens and in the wild.' The Alpine Garden Society offers grants to support research on alpine plants and their habitats. It has been supporting a conservation project at Haweswater in the Lake District since March 2017, working alongside the Royal Society for the Protection of Birds, United Utilities and Natural England to restore native alpine plants to the fells around Haweswater reservoir.

Conserving Genetic Diversity and Historical Interest

Selected cultivars of garden plants can be remarkably long-lived. Keeping old plants going is important to those for whom plants invoke memories. The French violet 'Marie Louise', dating to 1865, may remind someone of a much-loved grandmother. *Veronica prostrata* 'Warley Blue', named for Ellen Willmott's Essex garden, can demonstrate the value of continuity of horticultural history. Maintaining the genetic diversity of plants in cultivation has wider significance for their adaptability to climate change. The conservation charity Plant Heritage has a National Plant Collection scheme which aims to ensure that cultivated plants continue to be available to future generations for cultural, medical, culinary and aesthetic use. Plant Collection holders care for a registered and documented collection of a group of plants. Holders may be private individuals with a passion for a particular species or conservation bodies including botanic gardens, National Trust gardens, the Royal Horticultural Society (RHS) and specialist horticultural societies. The collections contribute to global efforts to halt loss of plant biodiversity. The National Collection of *Meconopsis* at Holehird Gardens in the Lake District, for example, contains approximately 80 per cent of the named species and cultivars of those blue Himalayan poppies that are listed in the RHS *Plant Finder*.

Even the National Plant Collections are reliant on enthusiastic individuals for their continuation. Private collectors may have to give up their plants if personal circumstances change. Staff turnovers or changes in focus at botanical institutions can lead to collections being lost. An example of this is the aubrieta, one of the most loved and widely grown of rockery plants, which was formerly held as a collection at the University of Leicester Botanic Garden. By 2020 it was heading Plant Heritage's list of missing genera. Aubrieta was named in 1763 in honour of the French botanical illustrator Claude Aubriet (1688–1743). He accompanied botanist Joseph Pitton de Tournefort on an expedition to the Middle East from 1700 to 1702, making drawings of the historical sites and flora of the region. On his return to Paris he was made 'Painter to the King' and painted twenty-four miniatures on vellum every year for thirty-five years. Most of these are still in the collection of the French National Museum of Natural History. In January 2024 there were twenty-one accepted species of aubrieta on the Kew list. They grow from south-eastern Europe across to Iran. Aubrieta is an easily grown, reliable alpine plant that is an early source of pollen for insects such as bees. It forms violet carpets of bloom that can cascade over rocks and spill from low walls. In cultivation many colour forms have been selected and there are cultivars with double flowers and those with variegated leaves. They certainly would make an interesting collection.

Aubrieta growing wild on Mount Parnassus, Greece, 2018.

Above: The former National Aubrieta Collection at Leicester Botanic Garden.

Below: The cultivar *Aubrieta* 'Elsie Cunnington' at Leicester.

Aubrieta 'Blue Cascade'.

The Use of Natural Stone

It is not just plants that people today are concerned about. When Reginald Farrer was writing his books in the early twentieth century, he advocated local waterworn limestone as the perfect stone for rock gardens. Professor John Stewart Parker, who was the director of Cambridge University Botanic Garden from 1996 to 2011, described how their limestone rock garden used about 900 tonnes of limestone pavement blocks from north Lancashire when it was created in the 1950s. Limestone pavements are level outcrops of exposed rock where the surface has been dissolved by water over millions of years so that it resembles paving blocks, called clints, with a pattern of crevices, known as grikes, between them. As well as their interest to geologists, limestone pavements provide a unique habitat for many unusual plants. They are irreplaceable landscapes, but only around 2,600 hectares remain in Britain, mainly in North Yorkshire, Cumbria and Lancashire. Small areas are found in Wales, Perthshire and the north west of Scotland. There is also pavement found in County Fermanagh in Northern Ireland and the well-known site at The Burren in Ireland.

Today limestone pavement heads the UK's list for conservation of threatened habitats. The best sites in England are covered by Limestone Pavement Orders, designed to

Limestone pavement at The Burren in Ireland. (Image Mary Bettini Blank/Pixabay)

stop damage to specially designated locations. Despite being protected areas, some pavements continue to be broken up and sold in garden centres as rockery stone. The Limestone Pavement Action Group was formed to discourage use of water-worn limestone in landscaping schemes and rockeries and to prevent the illegal trade in the rare rock. Builders of rock gardens certainly have many alternatives at their disposal. Stone availability varies. The Royal Horticultural Society recommends the use of local stone so that the garden looks in keeping with its surroundings. For those living in areas where stone is common, visiting a local quarry allows the selection of suitable rocks and reduces transportation concerns. However, some companies use more sustainable quarrying methods than others and transport of large, heavy rocks will always have some environmental impact.

Peat gardens became popular in the early twentieth century with peat blocks used instead of stone to create low walls and terraces. Peat blocks are light and easy to handle and permit the growth of acid-loving plants such as rhododendrons and trilliums. The peat garden at the Edinburgh Botanic Gardens was first developed in 1939, but the blocks degrade and have to be replaced every fifteen years or so. They were rebuilt in 2012 using peat blocks from a sustainable source in Scandinavia. Peat bogs are only slowly renewable resources as they gain less than a millimetre of depth a year and overharvesting in Europe has caused some peat wetlands to sustain serious damage. Peat disturbance also releases large amounts of carbon dioxide into the air. Compressed coir blocks are made from the

81

The peat garden at Utrecht Botanic Garden.

waste products of the coconut industry, but processing and transport issues means they still have ecological repercussions.

Salvaged or second-hand natural stone has been used for rock gardens for hundreds of years, although, again, ideas of what is an acceptable practice have changed. The best-known stone features at Wallington Hall in Northumberland are the four fabulous carved dragon heads which date from the sixteenth century. They were brought from Bishopsgate in London in 1760, as ballast in one of the coal-carrying ships of Sir Walter Blackett. However, the large standing stone near the east end of the China Pond in the grounds of the hall is considerably older. It is thought to have been moved there in the early eighteenth century from The Poind And His Man, a prehistoric site that lies between Shaftoe Crags and Bolam Lake to the south-east of Wallington. Another example of ancient stones being used as garden features occurred when Josiah Lane of Tisbury in Wiltshire was working on a landscaping scheme around Old Wardour Castle in 1792. He used stones from the castle ruins to build a grotto and created a small stone circle incorporating three standing stones removed from the Bronze Age stone circle at Tisbury. Of course, the moving of stones that were erected in prehistoric times would be considered shocking today. Lane's grotto is itself protected as a Schedule II building on the National Heritage List for England.

Above: Stone dragon heads at Wallington. (Image Nick/Pixabay)

Right: An inventive use of a broken pot makes an attractive exhibit using the high alpine *Androsace vandelli*.

Although natural stone, and especially stone with a history, is seen as the most desirable material, perhaps giving us an emotional link to our Stone Age ancestors, when this is unavailable gardeners through the ages have proved to be remarkably inventive. Reginald Malby (1882–1924) was a renowned photographer. His rock garden at Woodford in Essex was inspired by William Robinson's book *Alpine Flowers for Gardens*. As there was no stone quarried nearby he used roughly broken blocks of concrete to create the conditions required. His moraine bed was very successful and enabled him to grow treasured alpines such as the beautiful blue *Eritrichium nanum*. Malby wrote *The Story of My Rock Garden* in 1912. It demonstrated how it is possible to build an attractive rockery with crevices suitable for a range of interesting and beautiful plants in an ordinary suburban garden. He provided a month-by-month guide to flowers showing how he achieved a succession of flower from 1 January to 31 December, with his own photographs of *Ramonda myconi*, *Androsace studiosorum* 'Chumbyi', *Crocus versicolor* and *Campanula allionii*.

Some of the most inventive rock gardens found today are in the Netherlands, where Harry Jans' inspirational tufa walls demonstrate how to grow plants in small spaces and the gardeners at Utrecht Botanic Garden produce fascinating garden features from recycled materials. Utrecht has one of the largest rock gardens in Europe, covering almost 5 acres. The garden was constructed on the site of a disused fortress with stone imported from Belgium. Raised beds were built from 'Old Dutch' roof tiles which are grey and look like slate. Interesting planters have been made from broken ceramic drain pipes.

A raised planter in Amsterdam.

Above: Rock garden globes at Utrecht.

Below: A jackdaw enjoying the garden globes at Utrecht.

Above: *Primula marginata* planted in a globe.

Below: A drainage pipe planter at Utrecht Botanic Garden.

Petersen Rock Garden, 1987. (Image John Margolies/Library of Congress)

Three large spheres, ranging in height from 1.5 to 2 metres, were created in 1995–96 from recycled paving slabs and are planted with alpine plants including daphnes and *Haberlea rhodopensis*.

The 4-acre Petersen Rock Garden at Redmond in Oregon is a sculpture garden rather than a traditional alpine garden but demonstrates what an enthusiast can do with recycled materials. It was built by Rasmus Petersen, an immigrant from Denmark, who began constructing the garden in 1935 using rocks he found around the family home. In the tradition of model villages, he made highly detailed miniature buildings, including castles and churches and a 2-metre-high replica of the Statue of Liberty. The Rock Garden of Chandigarh in India has a similar eclectic theme. The work of Nek Chand (1924–2015), the garden began as a way for him to work through his grief at having to leave his childhood home due to the violence caused by the Partition of India in August 1947. His family moved to Chandigarh in 1955 when the city was being redesigned by the architect Le Corbusier. Chand collected materials, including rags, electrical waste and ceramics, from demolition sites around the city and used these to create a world of imaginary people and animals. In 1976 the park was inaugurated as a public space and it continues to be looked after since Chand's death by The Rock Garden Society. For Chand, the building of his garden was cathartic. There is an increasing body of research showing gardens and green spaces are associated with better physical, social and mental health.

Viewing flowers such as these *crocus goulimyi* from the Peloponnese in Greece can improve your wellbeing.

The Rock Garden as Therapy

In the second edition of her book *Notes on Nursing: What It Is, and What It Is Not*, published in 1860, Florence Nightingale wrote:

> I have seen, in fevers (and felt, when I was a fever patient myself), the most acute suffering produced from the patient (in a hut) not being able to see out of window, and the knots in the wood being the only view. I shall never forget the rapture of fever patients over a bunch of bright-coloured flowers. I remember (in my own case) a nosegay of wild flowers being sent me, and from that moment recovery becoming more rapid. People say the effect is only on the mind. It is no such thing. The effect is on the body, too. Little as we know about the way in which we are affected by form, by colour, and light, we do know this, that they have an actual physical effect.

The neurologist Dr Oliver Sacks agreed. In an excerpt from *Everything in Its Place* (2019), he described how an elderly lady with Parkinson's disease 'often found herself frozen, unable to initiate movement — a common problem for those with parkinsonism. But once we led her out into the garden, where plants and a rock garden provided a varied landscape, she was galvanized by this, and could rapidly, unaided, climb up the rocks and down again'. Sacks firmly believed in 'the restorative and healing powers of nature and gardens, even for those who are deeply disabled neurologically'.

One of the first purpose-built asylums in England for patients with mental illness was Brislington House in Bristol, opened in 1806 by Edward Long Fox, a Quaker with strong belief in the restorative power of nature. The landscaped grounds had a walled garden for the growing of fruit and vegetables and winding paths edged with rough rocks in the picturesque style. There was a grotto and a viewing platform on which was a stone table surrounded by a horseshoe-shaped bench ornamented by Sarsen stones. These encouraged patients to exercise in the fresh air and provided pleasing views in line with the belief that seeing objects of beauty could help to correct thought patterns.

Philanthropist Elizabeth Crichton (1779–1862) used her inheritance to fund the Crichton Royal Hospital. When opened in 1839 this was at the forefront of the humane and progressive treatment of people with mental health problems. The first medical superintendent, Dr William Alexander Francis Browne (1805–85), introduced a programme of activities and art therapy for patients. Both he and Crichton were firm believers in the therapeutic value of gardens and gardening. Extensive gardens were created in the grounds including a notable rock garden, with flights of steps and rock-topped arches. Dr George Watt (1851–1930), formerly Professor of Botany at Calcutta University, introduced many Indian plants, liaising with staff at the Royal Botanic Garden in Edinburgh to expand the plant collection. The crested iris (*Iris wattii*), native to Assam and western China, was named in his honour by Joseph Dalton Hooker. The hospital moved to new premises in 2012 but the rock garden survives under the care of the Crichton Trust gardeners.

Gardens are important for the health and mental well-being of staff as well as patients and many hospitals created gardens as places to promote rest and healing. A proposal for

Iris wattii commemorates Dr George Watt.

The Rock Garden, Hornsey Cottage Hospital.

Nurses in the rock garden at Hornsey Cottage Hospital.

a 'hospital for the poor' was first made at Hornsey in 1897 and the cottage hospital was opened in 1910. It was extended in 1924 as part of a War Memorial for those killed during the First World War. A nurses' home was built in 1930 and a children's ward opened in 1938. The rock garden created in the grounds provided a pleasing outdoor space in which people could relax.

During the twentieth century many hospital gardens were removed to make way for building expansion and car parking provision despite evidence of the positive influence of nature on health outcomes. Access to green spaces and trees may speed patient recovery actually saving the hospital money. The environmental psychologist Roger Ulrich showed that views of plants and trees from post-operative wards improves the mood of patients and reduces analgesic use, surgical complications and the length of stay. Gardening can be used as therapy with benefits beyond the medical. The National Health Service is increasingly using social prescribing (non-medical treatments) to tackle anxiety, loneliness and depression. Regular exercise is important for physical health and triggers activity within the brain that helps to protect and improve cognitive function and behaviour. Rock gardening is an activity that is accessible to all. Vita Sackville-West recommended in *In Your Garden* (1949) that:

> The rheumatic, the sufferers from lumbago, and the merely elderly, would all be well advised to try a little experiment in sink or trough gardening. By sink or trough we mean either those old-fashioned stone sinks now rejected in favour of glazed porcelain or aluminium; or the stone drinking-troughs with which pigs and cattle

The Christmas rose, *Helleborus niger*, in an old stone trough at East Lambrook Manor.

were once content before they had heard of concrete. Repudiated now by man and beast, they can be picked up in a house-breaker's yard for a few shillings.

Today stone troughs are highly prized commodities, no longer available for a few shillings, but her suggestions are still valid.

The young as well as the elderly benefit from time outdoors. The Kindness Rocks Project is a social media trend that encourages children to paint cobbles and leave them somewhere outdoors for others to find and collect. Photos of the painted rocks and hints of where to find them are shared online. Miniature rock gardens have been made in many towns using the painted rocks. It may not be alpine gardening in the purest sense, but it encourages children to be outdoors and may be the first step in stimulating an interest in gardening. The Scottish botanist Charlotte Murray wrote in *The British Garden* (1799), 'There is no other study or pursuit, so well adapted to expand the powers of the human mind, to elevate the sentiments, or amend the disposition, as that usually called the Study of Nature.'

In the First World War, British prisoners in the civilian internment camp at Ruhleben on the outskirts of Berlin in Germany started a gardening club when inmates were sent a gift of seeds by the Crown Prince of Sweden. Fruit and vegetables were particularly valued due to shortages of fresh produce, but flowers were also grown to cheer spirits

Children's Gardens, Sefton Park.

The children's gardens at Sefton Park in Liverpool included a planted rock as well as small conifers and statues of gnomes.

THE ROCKERY, SOUTH WALK. GILLINGHAM PARK, KENT. No. 617

The rockery at Gillingham Park in Kent was designed as an attractive and healthy place for children to enjoy fresh air and exercise.

Above: Miniature gardens occur among the exhibits at many alpine shows and may be a good way to encourage children to take an interest in alpine plants.

Right: A rock garden at the Ruhleben internment camp in Germany.

and remind them of home. They formed the Ruhleben Horticultural Society, which developed close links with the Royal Horticultural Society in London who sent seeds and plants to help them to develop a successful garden. Fortnightly lectures were arranged through the winter months to encourage a sense of community. A rockery, made using boulders unearthed on site and planted up with saxifrages and aubrieta, disguised the open drain that ran the length of the wash house, proving the positive benefits of rock gardens for the physical fitness and mental health of gardeners, even in such difficult environments.

Associations and Places to Visit

Alpine Garden Society – alpinegardensociety.net

Scottish Rock Garden Club – srgc.org.uk

Aysgarth Edwardian Rock Garden, Thornton Road, Leyburn, DL8 3AJ

Cambridge Botanic Garden, 1 Brookside, Cambridge CB2 1JE – botanic.cam.ac.uk

Chatsworth, Bakewell, Derbyshire, DE45 1PP – chatsworth.org

Chelsea Physic Garden, 66 Royal Hospital Road, London, SW3 4HS – chelseaphysicgarden.co.uk

Compton Acres, 164 Canford Cliffs Road, Poole, Dorset, BH13 7ES – comptonacres.co.uk

Doddington Place Gardens, near Sittingbourne, Kent, ME9 0BB – doddingtonplacegardens.co.uk

Royal Botanic Garden Edinburgh, 20a Inverleith Row, Edinburgh, EH3 5NZ – rbge.org.uk

Holehird Gardens, Patterdale Road, Windermere, LA23 1NP – holehirdgardens.org.uk

Kew Gardens, Richmond, London, TW9 3AE – kew.org

Leonardslee Gardens, Brighton Road, Lower Beeding, Horsham, RH13 6PP – leonardsleegardens.co.uk

Neston Road, Little Neston, Ness, CH64 4AY

Newby Hall, Ripon, North Yorkshire, HG4 5AE – newbyhall.com

Wisley RHS Garden, Woking, Surrey, GU23 6QB – rhs.org.uk

The National Botanic Gardens Glasnevin, 60 Glasnevin Hill, Glasnevin, Republic of Ireland – botanicgardens.ie

Bibliography

Amos, Robert, *International Conservation Law: The Protection of Plants in Theory and Practice* (Routledge: 2020)

Anderson, Rosemary, *Aysgarth Edwardian Rock Garden* (YPS Publishing: 2014)

Bednarik, Robert G., *Myths about Rock Art* (Archaeopress Archaeology: 2016)

Chesshire, Charles, *Japanese Gardening* (Aquamarine: 2006)

Clay, Sampson, *The Present-Day Rock Garden* (T. C. & E. C. Jack: 1937)

Elliott, Brent, 'The British rock garden in the twentieth century', *Occasional Papers from the RHS Lindley Library*, Volume 5 (March 2011)

Farrer, Reginald, *My Rock Garden* (Edward Arnold: 1907)

Farrer, Reginald, *The English Rock Garden* (T. C. & E. C. Jack: 1919)

Hitching, Claude and Lilly, Jenny, *Rock Landscapes: The Pulham Legacy* (Garden Art Press: 2012)

Hulme, Frederick E., *That Rock Garden of Ours* (T. Fisher Unwin: 1909)

Lawrence, Elizabeth, *A Rock Garden in the South* (Duke University Press: 1990)

Longstaffe-Gowan, Todd, *English Garden Eccentrics: Three Hundred Years of Extraordinary Groves, Burrowings, Mountains, and Menageries* (Paul Mellon: 2022)

Robinson, William, *Alpine Flowers for English Gardens* (John Murray: 1870)

Scott, Michael, *Mountain Flowers* (Bloomsbury: 2019)

Seth, Kenton and Spriggs, Paul, *The Crevice Garden* (Filbert Press: 2022)

Thomas, Graham Stuart, *The Rock Garden and Its Plants: from Grotto to Alpine House* (Timber Press: 2003)

Wilder, Louise Beebe, *Pleasures and Problems of a Rock Garden* (Doubleday & Doran, New York: 1928)

Wooster, David, *Alpine Plants: Figures and Descriptions of Some of the Most Striking and Beautiful of the Alpine Flowers* (Bell and Daldy: 1872)

Protection of Alpine Plants Science 3, No. 71 (1884), pp. 712–13